INNOVATIONS IN
PRACTICE
LEARNING

CRITICAL
SKILLS FOR
SOCIAL WORK

Other books you may be interested in:

Evidencing CPD – A Guide to Building Your Social Work Portfolio
By Daisy Bogg and Maggie Challis   ISBN 978-1-909330-25-2

Mental Health and the Criminal Justice System
By Ian Cummins   ISBN 978-1-910391-90-7

Modern Mental Health: Critical Perspectives on Psychiatric Practice
Edited by Steven Walker   ISBN 978-1-909330-53-5

Observing Children and Families: Beyond the Surface
By Gill Butler   ISBN 978-1-910391-62-4

Personal Safety for Social Workers and Health Professionals
By Brian Atkins   ISBN 978-1-909330-33-7

Positive Social Work: The Essential Toolkit for NQSWs
By Julie Adams and Angie Sheard   ISBN 978-1-909330-05-4

Practice Education in Social Work: Achieving Professional Standards
By Pam Field, Cathie Jasper and Lesley Littler   ISBN 978-1-909330-17-7

Psychosocial and Relationship-Based Practice
By Claudia Megele   ISBN 978-1-909682-97-9

Self-Neglect: A Practical Approach to Risks and Strengths Assessment
By Shona Britten and Karen Whitby   ISBN 978-1-912096-86-2

The Social Worker's Guide to the Care Act
By Pete Feldon   ISBN 978-1-911106-68-5

Starting Social Work: Reflections of a Newly Qualified Social Worker
By Rebecca Joy Novell   ISBN 978-1-909682-09-2

Understanding Substance Use: Policy and Practice
By Elaine Arnull   ISBN 978-1-909330-93-1

What's Your Problem? Making Sense of Social Policy and the Policy Process
By Stuart Connor   ISBN 978-1-909330-49-8

Working with Family Carers
By Valerie Gant   ISBN 978-1-912096-97-8

Titles are also available in a range of electronic formats. To order please go to our website www.criticalpublishing.com or contact our distributor NBN International, 10 Thornbury Road, Plymouth PL6 7PP, telephone 01752 202301 or email orders@nbninternational.com

CRITICAL
PUBLISHING

INNOVATIONS IN
PRACTICE
LEARNING

Edited by Sue Taplin

CRITICAL
SKILLS FOR
SOCIAL WORK

First published in 2018 by Critical Publishing Ltd

Copyright © 2018 Sue Taplin, Mark Doel, Caroline Hills, Jackie Plenty, Heidi Dix, Sarah Flanagan, Allan Norman, Sue Hollinrake, Gabi Hesk, Ian Mathews, Rachel Hunt, Su McCaughan, Andrea Stanley

British Library Cataloguing in Publication Data
A CIP record for this book is available from the British Library

ISBN: 978-1-912096-12-1

This book is also available in the following e-book formats:
MOBI ISBN: 978-1-912096-11-4
EPUB ISBN: 978-1-912096-10-7
Adobe e-book ISBN: 978-1-912096-09-1

The rights of Sue Taplin, Mark Doel, Caroline Hills, Jackie Plenty, Heidi Dix, Sarah Flanagan, Allan Norman, Sue Hollinrake, Gabi Hesk, Ian Mathews, Rachel Hunt, Su McCaughan and Andrea Stanley to be identified as the Authors of this work have been asserted by them in accordance with the Copyright, Design and Patents Act 1988.

Cover design by Out of House
Text design by Greensplash Limited
Project Management by Out of House Publishing
Printed and bound in Great Britain by 4edge, Essex

Critical Publishing
3 Connaught Road
St Albans
AL3 5RX

www.criticalpublishing.com

Paper from responsible sources

Contents

Meet the **editor**

Dr Sue Taplin

Sue is registered as a social worker in England and has a wealth of practice experience in palliative care and bereavement support. She has held a number of academic posts which have largely focused on service user and carer involvement and in the co-ordination of practice learning opportunities for students at both undergraduate and postgraduate levels.

In 2012 Sue was awarded a Professional Doctorate in Social Work from the University of East Anglia and she is a regular presenter at national and international conferences on her doctoral research as well as on numerous aspects of pedagogic practice.

Sue is currently Senior Lecturer in Social Work at Kingston and St George's, University of London.

Meet the contributors

Heidi Dix

Heidi Dix has been a qualified social worker since 1997 and has experience of both adult and children's services. She currently holds a part-time management role within Suffolk Youth Offending Service where she supports research-informed, relationship-based practice within the Service. Heidi is also a Lecturer in Social Work at the University of Suffolk where she teaches on a range of modules. As a practising social worker, Heidi is passionately committed to social justice and her interests include feminist social work, practice teaching and learning and co-production within the youth justice system.

Sarah Flanagan

Sarah is a Senior Lecturer at Leeds Trinity University. Sarah teaches on a cluster of programmes related to Children, Young People and Families. Her research interests include the relationship between employment and learning that occurs within formal institutions.

Gabrielle Hesk

Gabi Hesk works at the University of Salford as a Lecturer in Social Work on the Practice Learning and Admissions Team. Working in Health and Social Care for over 20 years in C&F positions, Gabi is registered with the HCPC and practises as an off-site practice educator and is active in practice as a Chair for a Fostering Panel. Gabi has a keen interest in experiential learning and a passion for community activism, which translate into a diverse range of research interests. Publications: https://usir.salford.ac.uk/view/authors/45988.html

Caroline Hills

Caroline has been an occupational therapist for over 30 years and has worked in the UK, Ireland and Australia as a clinician, manager and academic. Caroline is particularly interested in practice education, teaching and learning, interprofessional education, evidencing competence, and technology in practice. Her PhD thesis was entitled 'Are contemporary practice environments conducive to the learning needs and preferences of "Generation Y" Occupational Therapy students?' Caroline currently works in the occupational therapy programme at the National University of Ireland, Galway.

Sue Hollinrake

Dr. Sue Hollinrake is an Associate Professor and was Programme Lead for Social Work at the University of Suffolk until she (semi) retired in 2017. She had a long career in social work practice as a practitioner and manager before becoming an academic. Her teaching has covered professional values and social work with adults, and her research interests have focused on carers, older people and disabled people. Sue continues to publish on these topics.

Rachael Hunt

Rachael Hunt is the Practice Placement Co-ordinator for social work programmes at the University of Lincoln and has a wide range of responsibilities relating to placement management and provision. She has a number of research interests in practice learning, especially supporting students and practice educators with issues surrounding dyslexia.

Ian Mathews

Ian Mathews is a Senior Lecturer and Programme Leader in Social Work at the University of Lincoln and has been a qualified social worker since 1981. His areas of interest include spirituality, mental health and disability.

Su McCaughan

Su McCaughan is a Lecturer at the University of Salford in the Practice Learning and Admissions Team. She is a registered social worker with the Health Care Professions Council (HCPC) and an HCPC CPD assessor. Her practice career includes 20 years' experience in criminal justice.

Her teaching and research reflects a focus on practice education. She is an off-site practice educator and a Fellow of the Higher Education Academy. See the subject publications on her SEEK Profile: www.seek.salford.ac.uk/profiles/SMcCaughan.jsp

Allan Norman

Allan qualified as a social worker in 1990, and as a solicitor 10 years later. In addition to maintaining an independent social work practice, Allan trains and lectures on social work law, including contributing to qualifying and post-qualifying courses at the Universities of Birmingham, Sheffield and Warwick.

Jackie Plenty

After 25 years in social work practice and higher education Jackie has now retired to the North Norfolk coast where she continues to write. She feels honoured to have contributed to the careers of hundreds of social work students and practice educators including publishing numerous research articles, and is pleased to see this publication of the Problem-Based Capability Model aimed at assisting students and educators in frontline practice.

Andrea Stanley

Andrea Stanley is a Social Work Lecturer at the University of Salford and a member of the Practice Learning and Admissions Team. She is a registered social worker with the Health Care Professions Council (HCPC) and is actively involved as a practice educator. Prior to working for Salford University, Andrea held various posts within Mental Health Services and Adult Social Care and her teaching and research interests reflect this practice background.

Preface

Emeritus Professor Mark Doel

The wallpapers of practice education

Before you proceed to the excellent chapters that follow, I would like to invite you to pause and to consider the 'wallpaper' of practice learning. *Wallpaper* refers to the taken-for-granted background that is easily forgotten because it has become so familiar or contains challenges that we have chosen to neglect. Often it is only when we are taken out of our habitual circumstances that we become aware of wallpaper. Recently, for example, I went to a theatre in which all 600 members of the audience were Black, apart from me. In many situations, my Whiteness is near-invisible to me, like a white painting on a white wall, but when I am fortunate to have this contrast I can then become aware of my Whiteness.

Student learning can help practice teachers become aware of wallpaper. Suddenly, what has been the cosy, taken-for-granted backdrop to a professional world is scrutinised by a relative stranger, one who is licensed to ask questions.

In this Preface, I would like briefly to adopt the role of student and query some of the taken-for-granteds in practice learning. In doing this I will also 'problematise' them; in other words, raise the possibility that the wallpapers are not neutral, but conceal awkward challenges and conundrums that have been obscured. Here they are, then, four different kinds of wallpaper:

Generalist education in specialist settings – how to provide a general education in specialist practice contexts?

In some disciplines, for example, social work, students are experiencing a general education in their academic settings while being expected to learn about this professional practice in a particular and specialised setting. We take this as a given, yet it is a great challenge, not least for practice educators who must remind themselves that they are *educating* a social worker, not *training* a child protection worker/Cafcass worker/ mental health practitioner, etc. And yet, how capably the student can learn and practise as, for instance, a mental health practitioner, will be taken as an indicator of how capable they will be as a social worker.

It is quite complex, this idea that the student is learning the general from the specific – how, for instance, to write competent reports by using the specific example of what it is to write a competent report in this particular organisation. It is easy to forget that this move from general to specific, and back again, is the essence of practice learning. In the case of report writing, what are the core and essential skills of report writing that can be learned here in Agency A and that will transfer to report writing in Agencies B, C and D; and – just as importantly – what are the differences which will require adjustments when writing reports in those other agencies?

There have been some calls to specialise social work education, even at its basic level. It is my belief that if this is ever allowed to happen it will be the end of the social work profession as we know it. A shared education in social work theory and practice, and a common understanding of its value base, is an essential component of a unified profession. Already 'social worker' is disappearing from job titles, though the requirement for a qualification as a social worker remains. It is critical to maintain the integrity of the social work profession through a common, general education. We need to address the conundrum of a general education learned and tested in a specific setting as a positive – an enlightening pedagogical challenge. If we allow it to become wallpaper, we expose it to the danger that it might at some point be stripped off entirely, with dire consequences for the profession.

Timelines – how to accommodate the fact that students learn at different speeds?

Students, practice educators and tutors all operate within a system that assumes everyone learns at the same pace. We pay a kind of lip service to students as adult learners, that they start from different places and have varying learning needs, yet the structures that have been created scarcely accommodate this fact.

If we were to take a cohort of 100 students and ask them how long it took them to pass the driving test (in terms of the number of assessment events – ie driving tests – and also the number of months and years between the first lesson and the successful outcome) we could expect an enormous range. Yet we will expect each of these same 100 students to learn to practise a much more complex set of skills over a common period of time. There are some small adjustments possible through extended placements and the like, but this does not adequately reflect the reality of different students' learning needs and paces.

It is taken for granted that all the students in any one cohort are expected to achieve an acceptable level of ability within the same period – two, three or four years. The fact that it is difficult to see an alternative or to engineer some wiggle room has led us to treat this conundrum as wallpaper (to mix metaphors, just another chord in the background noise), so that one of the biggest challenges in professional education – how to help different learners reach the finishing line all at the same time – is obscured and neglected. The fact that it is difficult to imagine an alternative should not lead us to ignore the challenge. In this new light, we should marvel that the number of students who do not cross the finishing line is as small as it is.

Congruency – how to achieve a correspondence between what is learned (and assessed) and the methods used to promote the learning and make the assessment?

If you were asked to devise a programme of learning and assessment for a student pianist, without doubt it would centre on a piano. The student might discuss notation and interpretation and write essays on musical theory, but by far the largest part of their learning would take place around a piano, with the piano teacher playing or listening. Social work is not piano playing, but service users might rightly expect a qualified social worker to have had many hours 'playing' in sight of their teacher and, indeed, to have spent many hours watching their teacher in practice. They might be surprised to learn that it is possible for a student social worker to qualify with only three or four direct observations of their practice as a social worker per placement; and with no requirement at all that they have seen their practice teacher, their maestro, 'playing'.

This under-observation of student social workers, and the privileging of the discussion of practice over the practice of practice, is troubling to me. However, more troubling is the fact that it gets so little attention. It is another of the wallpapers of practice education; so prevalent and taken for granted that it is no longer remarkable or remarked upon.

Of course, I know that some practice educators have considerable hands-on contact with their student's practice and we need more research to know just how much direct time together is the norm. I suspect, though, that the norm is quite low as a percentage of the student's time on placement. I do not seek to devalue the worth of supervision discussions, of reflective diaries and meetings with colleagues and professionals, but I do think the profession needs more discussion about the value of direct hands-on teaching and learning and methods of achieving this. We have much to learn from pianists.

Sampling – how to select what learning and assessment is most significant?

It is not possible to learn about everything, nor to assess everything. In effect, practice educators are sampling all the time – in the tasks that students are given to help their learning and in the ways that are used to test their capabilities. Yet we seldom refer explicitly to sampling or the best methods to use to achieve the most effective and efficient sampling. What research evidence do we have that guides us to the core tasks and abilities that, if acquired, provide a good indication that other capabilities flow from them?

I have often found it helpful to look outside social work for analogous activities – if you like, ways to put yourself in a new situation to better see the wallpaper. For instance, if you were a knitting teacher, at what point would you feel confident that the student knitter had demonstrated sufficient skills? Once the basic knit stitch had been acquired you would want to see evidence of the student's ability to reproduce this stitch sufficiently to produce a garment, such as a scarf. The skills of 'casting on', which allow the subsequent knit stitches, would need to be demonstrated, too, so that the student could start off a garment, as well as finish it. Once these stitch techniques had been learned and demonstrated, at what point would you infer that the student could reproduce these skills sufficiently to 'pass'? If the student can knit with red wool, it is reasonable to infer that they can do the same with blue wool, but how about the thickness of the wool and size of the needles, different stitch and pattern styles – how many different factors would you introduce to test the student's skills and what would these be?

Sampling in practice education is no different; what are the 'stitches', 'patterns' and 'garments' of social work and how do we sample from the student's work to make a judgement? We *do* sample, but it is rarely conceptualised as *sampling.* Practice educators are not taught sampling theory and we have little research evidence that if the student is competent at N, there is a strong probability (or not) that they are also competent at B, Q and Z. Perhaps because this research evidence is not easy to generate, sampling has been consigned to the status of wallpaper – an all-present and necessary feature of practice learning and teaching, but unrecognised, implicit and untested.

Students have the opportunity and the licence to point to the wallpaper and to ask questions about it. Practice educators have a responsibility to uncover wallpaper so that the fundamental conundrums of practice learning can benefit from our collective gaze, instead of being obscured by familiarity.

One of the significant aspects of the methods and models in the subsequent chapters in this book is that they are not wallpaper; they are explicitly articulated models that have been tried and tested and seen to work. As such I know you will find them interesting and practically useful in your own practice learning and teaching.

Professor Mark Doel is Emeritus Professor at Sheffield Hallam University

Editor's introduction: Is there a Plan B?

Dr Sue Taplin

As is so often the case in practice – and in practice placements – the writing of this book did not go to plan.

Conceived initially as a jointly authored book to be written by two university practice learning co-ordinators, along the way there have been many changes – in authors and their job titles, in publisher, in content – to the extent that what you now are about to read is almost unrecognisable when compared to the original plan.

At many stages in the past three years it would have been easy to admit defeat – but my fundamental belief in the importance of this project, as well as the encouragement of friends and colleagues in the field of practice learning – has enabled me to produce what, in hindsight, I believe to be a far better text than was originally planned. The need to respond to change, including the many changes that have taken place in the landscape of social work and social work training, has enabled me to move from the position of author to that of editor, and thus to broaden the scope of the book to include examples of best practice from a variety of contributors both within and outside of social work, whose different styles of teaching and writing offer something to a wider audience than would originally have been the case.

As editor of this textbook, I have had the opportunity to reflect on the contemporary landscape of health and social care and to ensure that the book responds to the many changes and challenges that practitioners are now facing. Selecting and working with the contributors has given me the opportunity to showcase some of the most exciting and innovative models in practice education.

In Chapter 1, while recognising that our learners may begin their studies at any stage of adulthood, Hills offers some interesting observations on the practice learning needs of our most recent generation of learners – Generation Y – and the significance of viewing differences in learning styles through a generational lens.

In the next three chapters, practitioners and academics explore innovative methods and models which they have successfully applied to the arena of practice learning, and provide honest and reflective accounts of the challenges they have encountered in so doing. In Chapter 2, Plenty and Dix introduce the Problem-Based Capability Model as a way of encouraging creativity in exploring casework in accordance with the requirements of the Professional Capabilities Framework. In Chapter 3, Dix explores the complex process of supervision, suggesting ways in which it can become a creative forum for shared learning, as well as a means of assessment and support, and in the Chapter 4, Flanagan provides a practical insight into the place of storytelling in facilitating adult learning.

In Chapter 5, Norman succeeds in bringing to life a subject seldom explored in the context of work-based learning – the application of law to practice – and this is brought further into focus in Chapter 6 with Hollinrake's focus on values and ethics, which stresses the fundamental importance of developing skills in anti-oppressive practice.

The final chapters derive from practice educators' experiences of working with students to explore issues of potential discrimination in practice learning, with Chapter 7 addressing the experiences of Black students and Chapter 8 that of students with dyslexia. Both chapters provide honest reflections and insights from practice of their learning in these areas.

From initial training to professional development in frontline practice, the models demonstrated in the chapters which follow can be used both to enhance skills and also to challenge established patterns of working, to develop relationships between supervisors and practitioners at all levels of experience and to bring practice issues alive, not only in the classroom but also in practice in a supervision setting.

The models presented within this book have been proved by the authors to be both practical and effective; they have come from direct experience and demonstrate ways in which to rehearse and develop skills that will increase self-confidence and effective practice. As such, they can provide practitioners with the necessary compass with which to navigate the unchartered territory of human experience, better to comprehend not only the complex lives of the people we are as practitioners, but also to intervene more effectively in the lives of the service users and carers with whom we work.

So – is there a Plan B? In good social work practice, as in writing a textbook, the answer must be 'yes' – there is always an alternative: and if you embrace the challenge and are open and responsive to change the end result may be very different – but infinitely better – than your original plan.

Dr Sue Taplin

Chapter 1 | Generation Y: Reflections on our current generation of learners

Caroline Hills

All supervisors want their student(s) to develop the requisite skills, attitudes and knowledge that are essential for graduating with competency in their profession. Indeed, taking a student on placement is indicative of the supervisor's desire and commitment to mentoring and guiding the student towards the attainment of these essential skills and attributes. From the student's perspective, the most successful placements are those in which the student has had a good relationship with their educator and have been facilitated towards independence with some degree of autonomy in that particular work setting. While many studies have reported that the most preferred characteristics of the supervisor are that they are enthusiastic and approachable (Francis et al, 2016; Perram et al, 2016), students have also used the term 'belonging' in their descriptions of successful placements (Hills et al, 2016a). 'Belonging' is the human need to be accepted, recognised, valued and appreciated by a group (Maslow, 1943). Social scientists have defined 'belongingness' as a feeling of being respected and appreciated and having an integral role in an environment, which is achieved through participation in that setting (Anant, 1969). People who experience 'belongingness' feel they 'fit in' as they feel needed, valued and accepted (Hagerty et al, 1992). However, it is not only the relationship with the supervisor that facilitates this essential feeling; it is also being part of the team, feeling like a colleague – and for students it has been reported as a prerequisite to both enabling and optimising their learning (Levett-Jones and Lathlean, 2008).

In order to create a feeling of 'belongingness', the placement must begin with consideration of the student's attributes in relation to their learning needs and preferences. This recognises that we do not all learn in the same way. To begin with acknowledging difference enables individualised learning approaches to be adopted. Considerations such as learning style, gender, cultural and family background, or the presence of a health condition or disability, may be important starting points, in addition to the student's life and previous work experience relevant to the area of practice (Larkin and Hamilton, 2010). However, age or 'generation' has been noted as another factor that can affect student learning in placement (Larkin and Hamilton, 2010).

In her book *Generation Me* (2006), Jean Twenge describes the fundamental premise which underpins a generational perspective:

Everyone belongs to a generation. Some people embrace it like a warm familiar blanket, while others prefer not to be lumped in with their age mates. Yet, like it or not, when you are born dictates the culture you will experience. This includes the highs and lows of pop culture, as well as world events, social trends, economic realities, behavioural norms, and ways of seeing the world. The society moulds you when you are young and stays with you the rest of your life.

(Twenge, 2006, p 2)

Defining differences in generational cohorts was first proposed by the German sociologist Karl Mannheim in the 1950s. Mannheim (1952) postulated that each generation has a similar worldview due to exposure to common historical and social events during their formative years. Every member of a specific generation will not have experienced the same life events, but they will have a shared awareness which creates a type of 'generational personality'. This is attributed to belonging to the same generational age group and sharing a common location in the social and historical world. Subsequently, generational classifications have been developed by social commentators in westernised countries. These include the 'GI Generation' (born 1901–1924); the 'Silent Generation' (1925–1942); the 'Baby Boomers' (1943–1960); 'Generation X' (1961–1981); 'Generation Y' or 'Millennials' (1982–2002) and 'Generation Z' from 2003 onwards (Prendergast, 2009). Supporters of a generational perspective have argued that each generation's personality has a unique set of characteristics, developed as a result of their experiences during their formative years. These characteristics comprise beliefs, values, attitudes and expectations, which affect behaviour in general, as well as in educational and work settings (Boudreau, 2009; Lavoie-Tremblay et al, 2010).

Foster's (2013) analysis of the narrative discourse of workers confirmed that being part of one generation or commenting on other generations is a reality in contemporary society. For example, in this author's research, participants used language such as 'that generation' or 'the younger generation' and 'my generation', when discussing approaches to doing things differently in the workplace. However, many qualified these stereotypical comments by stating that not everyone of a particular generation fits the generalisation. Foster (2013, p 211) concluded that a generational perspective:

... proves particularly useful when people attempt to understand and convey perceived differences in older and younger contemporaries, and the social, cultural, and especially technological changes affecting their lives. It is a one-word lens through which both choice and determinism are rendered visible in the lives of others.

Table 1.1 Societal influences during the formative years of generations

	Baby Boomers (1943–1960)	**Generation X (1961–1981)**	**Generation Y (1982–2002)**
Notable occurrences	Civil rights movement	Rise of mass media and consumerism, end of Cold War	Globalisation, digital age, age of terrorism
Major influences	Family and education	Media, AIDS, nuclear disasters as well as family and education	Witness the growth of millionaires. Digital explosion. Family major influence. 'You are special'.
Entertainment	Television	Multiple TV channels, VCR, Nintendo, cinema	YouTube, live streaming, multiple media and technologies. Social media.
Communication and technology	Touch-tone phones, calculators	Mobile phones, beepers, laptops, email	More complex mobile technologies, WiFi, social media, creation of apps, more interactive video gaming and computer programs. Most homes own a computer.
Spending styles	Buy now pay later – with plastic	More cautious –pessimistic Security	Growth in designer labels and personalised items, ie phone covers
Value	Regularity, predictability	Fun, want challenges	Fun but want to achieve
Work ethic	'It pays to work hard' – workaholics	Satisfying teamwork	Likes teamwork but wants to achieve. May have multiple careers.

(Adapted from Prendergast, 2009)

> ## Task 1.1
>
> Define which generation you are from.
>
> Do you think those from older generations have different values from you? Consider choice of food, management of money, work-life balance, life or work expectations, use of technology, parenting styles or attitude to diversity. Were there any behaviours that you consider acceptable that older generations would not have considered to be acceptable?
>
> Think about having a conversation about when you were young. What would you discuss when reminiscing about your formative years with peers: music? films? TV? toys or gadgets? clothes or fashion? social life? food? Or would you consider world events, politics, or national disasters? Consider the social structures experienced by those from the generation before yours. Do you think that there are differences? Are some of your values different as a result of these experiences?
>
> Now think of younger generations: do their values differ from your own?

In the main, there are three generations in the workplace, each having different learning preferences generated from their experiences in their formative years.

Any one of these generations could be a supervisor or a student but it is Generation Y who are given most consideration in the literature as they comprise the majority of the current student population.

Generation Y: Who are they?

'Generation Y' individuals grew up in prosperous times and have experienced the introduction and wide dissemination of technology. This is claimed to have resulted in a generation of people who are independent, 'techno-savvy', entrepreneurial, flexible and hard-working (Tulgan and Martin, 2001). Also known as the 'Trophy Generation' (no one loses and everyone receives a trophy just for participating), they have been rewarded for effort rather than for performance. This group therefore are said to be a confident generation with a desire for praise and positive feedback (Crampton and Hodge, 2009). These messages are considered to have resulted in a generation who are emotionally 'needy', particularly at work, but who can also be overconfident in estimating their abilities (Crumpacker and Crumpacker, 2007; Shaw and Fairhurst,

Table 1.2 The learning differences between three generations

Baby Boomers (1943–1960)	Generation X (1961–1981)	Generation Y (1982–2002)
Strong work ethic; come prepared to the learning opportunity.	Want to learn usable skills. Value knowledge access over knowledge memorisation.	Experts in searching and accessing information, but not necessarily in analysing or synthesising the information.
May prefer more traditional methods of learning rather than a self-taught module. Will learn what the educator wants them to learn.	Want things presented in a straightforward manner. Want to learn only relevant information to the work or to pass a course.	Want to take on challenging tasks in their learning environment (thus may appear arrogant if the instruction is vague).
May be less comfortable with technology but are conscientious and accept help (digital immigrant).	Enjoy flexibility in learning, eg self-directed modules (digital native).	Are computer 'savvy' and use technology whenever possible (digital native).
Learn best when experience can be integrated with subject matter.	Want learning to be directly relevant to their work tasks. Don't want to learn something just for the sake of learning.	Expect immediate feedback on their work as they are accustomed to information access 24/7. Need praise for work well done.
Anticipate a slower-paced and more formal introduction to the training and rationale for it – like to have a hard copy.	Want to learn in the easiest and quickest way possible.	Need to feel a sense of achievement. Want goals and rules to be transparent. Prefer experiential activities.

(Adapted from The Health Education and Training Institute, 2012)

2008). However, Howe and Strauss (2000) contend that this also translates into optimism for their future, calling them *the next great generation*. In one study, placement supervisors reported on their positive attributes, indicating that Generation Y students are not intimidated by hierarchy. They were seen as articulate, assertive, confident, energetic, enthusiastic 'go-getters' who are innovative, adapt well to change and will make a difference to future practice (Hills et al, 2015).

These positive characteristics have been attributed to the parenting styles experienced by Generation Y. Parents have micromanaged their Generation Y children's time by organising their out-of-school activities and social life. They did this in part as a response to 'stranger danger' but also to ensure that their children's life experiences were positive and fruitful for their academic and social development. Thus the involvement of parents extends into their children's lives at college and into employment, with some authors noting that some parents contact lecturers and managers to advocate for, or discuss, their children's (now adults) needs. They are reported to be the most wanted generation due to the increased availability of contraception and abortion and a number of social commentators have agreed that Generation Y perceive themselves as special, but this has also been interpreted as being self-absorbed and narcissistic (Twenge and Campbell, 2008; Twenge and Foster, 2010). They have received consistent and compelling messages from parents and the media that they can achieve what they want to achieve, that nothing is impossible and that they must follow their dreams. However, this parental involvement has also been reported to have put pressure on students to achieve, with one author noting that Generation Y can become 'trophy children', with parents boasting about their children's attainments. This pressure, as well as that of social media, is said to have contributed to the increased anxiety and depression that is reported in this younger cohort. For students on placement, educators may witness a different attitude to both work and learning, as this group may demonstrate more selfish and self-entitled behaviours but also a well-adjusted work-life balance, leaving work on time with their own family being their priority. Rickes (2009) suggests that this model of parenting has resulted in a cohort that will socialise more with their parents and even 'boomerang' back to live with parents after college. Twenge (2006) reported that this return to living at home was delaying maturation to adulthood and one Australian author coined the term 'kid-adults' due to the number of Australian Generation Y young people who were still living at home (Mackay, 2007). Huntley (2006) suggested that this was less of a personal choice and more of a financial one. She argued that inflation has exceeded the cost of living and salaries have not risen at the same rate, thus members of Generation Y had been denied the opportunity to buy their own homes. Therefore, it is contended that other markers of adulthood such as marriage and children are delayed, resulting in a generation of people who can be flexible but who may also be insecure.

Technology in all its forms has been deemed as having most influence in the lives of this younger generation as it is used for leisure, work, friendship, relationships, banking and shopping. Rickes (2009) reported that for this cohort technology is a necessity as *omnipresent and mundane as a toaster'* (p 8). This is reflected in the application of the label 'digital natives' with older generations being called 'digital immigrants' (Prensky, 2001). However, while the use of technology has been credited with enhancing practice skills, it has also raised concerns for students on placement as having contributed to poor writing and spelling ability, poor professional behaviour and concern for ethical practice on social media, inappropriate use of mobile technologies in the workplace and a reluctance to critically evaluate the reliability of information gained via web searching. There are also other consequences for this reliance on technology, one of these being that students may not be confident in communicating by phone as they prefer to text. Another is that they can become easily bored in the workplace due to the lack of opportunity for connectivity, gaming and technological stimulation.

This is summarised in a Generation Y blog:

You see, the thing is I'm not a slacker. I'm really not. And it pisses me off when people assume that I am. It's just that I don't give, I can't give, 100% to something that doesn't interest me or when I'm not engaged. I love being busy! I live for it. In my ideal job, I love it so much that I have to answer e-mails while taking a shower. While getting a pedicure, while in my car (STOPPED at a red light, of course) or even (because my passion for my job goes beyond ALL things), while watching Gossip Girl! I LOVE working. It's what keeps me going. So I need a job that gives me that motivation to engage.

(Cruz, 2012)

Blashki et al (2007) argue that Generation Y is flexible, adaptable and spontaneous with an increased disposition towards participative behaviours and multitasking, but only if the task is interesting and engages them. However, Willingham (2010) refuted the claim that multitasking is essential for Generation Y learning or work, reporting that cognitively a person cannot switch between two tasks and do them well. In respect to placement, the question of how to engage this group in seemingly boring and mundane tasks is relevant, as many of these tasks are an essential part of practice. Students may be reluctant to engage in tasks that do not give them the opportunity to develop and 'shine'. They are said to be 'assessment-driven' and their educational experience has taught them to focus on 'ticking the boxes' on marking grids and assessment matrices, rather than engaging in the deep learning necessary for successful practice learning (Keating et al, 2009).

The Generation Y student

Due to these generational characteristics, 'Generation Y' students have been identified as having different expectations and learning styles to those of previous generations (Oblinger, 2003; Twenge, 2009). Indeed, Prensky (2001) argued that significant changes are required in tertiary education as *'today's students are no longer the people our educational systems were designed to teach'* (p 1). In Australia, Hills et al (2012) investigated occupational therapy supervisors' views on Generation Y students and found that most considered that 'Generation Y' students exhibited many of the classic generational personality traits. These included being techno-savvy, overconfident, easily bored, in need of constant feedback and praise, and having a different more casual communication style which was sometimes interpreted as a lack of professionalism. They also appeared more self-focused than client-focused, which was criticised by supervisors. Supervisors however praised their technological ability and considered that this skill will benefit the future of the profession. Concern was expressed regarding Generation Y students' apparent overconfidence resulting in a 'skimming' approach to reasoning and decision-making in their rush to get to the end point, as well as difficulty in accepting negative feedback. This survey was replicated with another group of supervisors in a different part of Australia and similar themes arose, with the additional observation that students' technological ability indicated that they are skilled in searching out evidence-based practice, which was valued by supervisors (Hills et al, 2015).

A generational cautionary tale

Before proceeding to identifying strategies to facilitate learning for cohorts of Generation Y students, there has to be a word of caution. Of course, not every student will be the same. Taking a generational perspective can be seen as unhelpful stereotyping and a form of moral panic that serves the agenda of some universities in explaining why the 'younger' student is not accepting of their traditional and outdated ways of learning (Bennett et al, 2008; Sternberg, 2012). All these criticisms may be true. However, taking a generational perspective can alert the supervisor and student to one explanation of different attitudes and approaches to learning. It can facilitate a conversation. It aims to create an awareness of possible differences. It alerts both parties to the possibility of generational reasons for difference or dissonance on placement. Indeed, you may come across a 'Baby Boomer' supervisor who is more technologically competent than a Generation Y student, or an underconfident Generation Y supervisor with an overconfident Baby Boomer student. Like learning styles and other mechanisms of getting to know your student it is a highlighter, not a predictor of difference. It stimulates an understanding or provides a possible explanation.

With this in mind, below is some guidance on practice learning with Generation Y, which may be of equal relevance to other generations but has been generated from investigating Generation Y students' teaching and learning preferences on placement (Hills et al, 2016a).

Welcoming the student

It is crucial to welcome the student to the setting and the team but also to be clear about expectations of professional behaviour from the first day of placement onwards. This might include dress code, acceptable language, work hours and breaks, use of mobile phones and access to the computer. These are important as role modelling alone may not be sufficient to ensure that the student is aware of required behaviours in the agency. Once it is clear, the student will appreciate the opportunity to demonstrate that they can achieve these standards. Remember that they want to be part of the whole team, so ensure everyone is part of the welcoming environment.

Getting to know the student

Students want supervisors who want to get to know them, as a person, as a learner and as a colleague. This is an ongoing process throughout the placement and is a reciprocal relationship. Students value those educators who share the challenges they experienced when they were students. They want the supervisor to acknowledge and build on their existing skills and knowledge. So, start with their needs and expectations of the placement. Competency assessment forms provide examples of what they are expected to demonstrate by the end of the placement. This will help the student to focus – but it is important to ensure that routine and mundane tasks are included. Identifying special projects for the student to complete may be a successful strategy for them to showcase their learning and provides an opportunity for them to achieve something particular that may contribute to the team.

Developing competence

'Learning by doing' is not a new concept as it is embedded in almost all learning theories. However, developing competence is more than completing a task to a practice standard or competency; the student must also be able to 'think' to a practice standard. According to Moore (2012), Generation Y students may expect the supervisor to have all the answers and to provide exceptionally clear direction. This group want the educator to talk through their thinking so they can have insight into practice problem-solving and decision-making. But for the student to develop their thinking, they need to be encouraged and facilitated to explore the ambiguity and uncertainties of practice. The student needs to be able to discuss their work with the educator so that the educator can agree or disagree, debate, explore and analyse, confirm or deny the accuracy of their practice thinking. Without 'talking' the work, there may be frustration in that the student considers they have completed the task (ticked the box) to standard, when in fact they failed to notice some crucial non-verbal cues that would require further investigation. As Generation Y are goal orientated, I recommend including aspects of 'talking' the work in weekly supervision sessions. This will motivate the student to develop the important skill of practice thinking, while also meeting their need for clarity of expectations of performance.

Feedback

The preference for feedback and praise in this generation is well documented, as is the fact that they may not respond well to negative feedback. Members of this generation appear to want as much feedback as possible – after an event, at the beginning or end of the day and in weekly supervision. But they can also be seen as goal-orientated achievers. Students have indicated that they want to be given the opportunity to self-evaluate before being given feedback so that they can 'rank' their own progression towards competency (Hills et al, 2016b). They also want 'pointers to improve' from the educator. In effect, feedback is less 'back' and more 'forward'. To feed-forward removes the need for 'negative' feedback, which can lead to emotional responses from both supervisor and student. To feed-forward means there is a plan of what needs to be done differently next time and this can be proposed by the student and confirmed or refined by the educator. 'Empty' praise, ie that which is not deserved, is not valued by students, so use praise only when deserved and required. However, praise or feed-back from others, including other team members and service users, is highly valued and should be encouraged as ultimately it is this that confirms that the student has achieved a feeling of 'belonging' to the team or service.

Use of technology

Technology is part of everyone's life and while you may need to give ethical guidance on use of social networking sites and appropriate use of mobile technologies, careful use of technology is to be encouraged. Moore (2012) reported on various ways in which technology can be used in social work practice. I am certainly aware of students using their mobile phone to look up new terms or diagnoses but this may be problematic if this has not been agreed with the supervisor, who may be thinking that the student is using their phone for personal use. Technology can enhance learning and advance practice, and Generation Y may be just the group to lead these types of developments.

Conclusion

Being a facilitator of student learning on placement means being student centred. This chapter has considered the relevance of a generational perspective to facilitating students' learning. A skilled facilitator starts with the students' needs rather than those of the supervisor. A generational perspective should not be based on the notion of stereotype but rather encourages a more nuanced consideration of difference. 'Generation' is a lens through which to consider differences in attitudes, behaviours and ways of learning that may be particular to each generational group. Successful placements invariably conclude with the student feeling that they are a valued team member and colleague and that they are 'part of' the service and their profession. Awareness of generational issues may be one contributing factor in ensuring that this goal is achieved.

References

Anant, A (1969) A Cross-Cultural Study of Belongingness, Anxiety and Self-Sufficiency. *Acta Psychologia*, 31: 385–93.

Bennett, S, Maton, K and Kervin, L (2008) The 'Digital Natives' Debate: A Critical Review of the Evidence. *British Journal of Educational Technology*, 39(5): 775–86. doi:10.1111/j.1467-8535.2007.00793.x

Blashki, K, Nichol, S, Jia, D and Prompramote, S (2007) The Future Is Old: Immersive Learning with Generation Y Engineering Students. *European Journal of Engineering Education*, 32(4): 409–20.

Boudreau, M L (2009) Is There a Generation Gap in Occupational Therapy? *Occupational Therapy Now*, 11(2): 16–18.

Crampton, S M and Hodge, J W (2009) Generation Y: Unchartered Territory. *Journal of Business and Economics Research*, 7(4): 1–6.

Crumpacker, M and Crumpacker, J M (2007) Succession Planning and Generational Stereotypes: Should HR Consider Age-Based Values and Attitudes a Relevant Factor or a Passing Fad? *Public Personnel Management*, 36(4): 349–69.

Cruz, K (2012) *Gen Y Girl*. [online] Available at: www.lostgenygirl.com/were-not-lazy-were-just-bored-out-of-our-fing-minds (accessed 23 June 2018).

Francis, A, Hills, C, MacDonald-Wicks, L, Johnston, C, James, D, Surjan, Y and Warren-Forward, H (2016) Characteristics of an Ideal Practice Educator: Perspectives from Practice Educators in Diagnostic Radiography, Nuclear Medicine, Nutrition and Dietetics, Occupational Therapy and Physiotherapy and Radiation Therapy. *Radiography*, 22(4): 287–94. doi: doi:10.1016/j.radi.2016.04.001

Hagerty, B, Lynch-Sauer, J, Patusky, K, Bouwsema, M and Collier, P (1992) A Sense of Belonging: A Vital Mental Health Concept. *Archives of Psychiatric Nursing*, 6(3): 172–7.

Health Education and Training Institute (2012) *The Learning Guide: A Handbook for Allied Health Professionals Learning in the Workplace*. Sydney, NSW, Australia: HETI.

Higgs, J (2013) Professional Socialisation, in Loftus, S, Gerzina, T, Higgs, J, Smith M and Duffy E (eds) *Educating Health Professionals* (pp 83–92). Rotterdam, the Netherlands: Sense.

Hills, C, Boshoff, K, Gilbert-Hunt, S, Ryan, S and Smith, D R (2015) The Future in Their Hands: The Perceptions of Practice Educators on the Strengths and Challenges of 'Generation Y' Occupational Therapy Students. *The Open Journal of Occupational Therapy*, 3(4): Article 6. doi:10.15453/2168–6408.1135

Hills, C, Levett-Jones, T, Warren-Forward, H and Lapkin, S (2016a) Teaching and Learning Preferences of 'Generation Y' Occupational Therapy Students in Practice Education. *International Journal of Therapy & Rehabilitation*, 23(8): 371–79. doi:10.12968/ijtr.2016.23.8.371

Hills, C, Levett-Jones, T, Lapkin, S and Warren-Forward, H (2016b) Generation Y Occupational Therapy Students' Views and Preferences about the Provision of Feedback During Clinical Practice Education. *Focus on Health Care Education: A Multi-Disciplinary Journal*, 17(2): 32–47.

Hills, C, Ryan, S, Smith, D R and Warren-Forward, H (2012) The Impact of "Generation Y" Occupational Therapy Students on Practice Education. *Australian Occupational Therapy Journal*, 59(2): 156–63. doi:10.1111/j.1440-1630.2011.00984.x

Hills, C, Ryan, S, Warren-Forward, H and Smith, D R (2013) Managing 'Generation Y' Occupational Therapists: Optimising Their Potential. *Australian Occupational Therapy Journal*, 60(4): 267–75. doi:10.1111/1440-1630.12043

Keating, J, Dalton, M and Davidson, M (2009) Assessment in Clinical Education, in Delaney, C and Molloy, E (eds) *Clinical Education in the Health Professions* (pp 147–72). Chatswood, NSW, Australia: Elsevier.

Larkin, H and Hamilton, A (2010) Making the Most of Your Fieldwork Opportunity, in Stagnitti, K, Schoo, A and Welch, D (eds) *Clinical and Fieldwork Placement* (pp 159–70). Melbourne, Australia: Oxford University Press.

Lavoie-Tremblay, M, Leclerc, E, Marchionni, C and Drevniok, U (2010) The Needs and Expectations of Generation Y Nurses in the Workplace. *Journal for Nurses in Staff Development*, 26(1): 2–10. doi:10.1097/NND.0b013e3181a68951

Levett-Jones, T and Lathlean, J (2008) Belongingness: A Prerequisite for Nursing Students' Clinical Learning. *Nurse Education in Practice*, 8: 103–11.

Mackay, H (2007) *Advance Australia ... Where?* Sydney, Australia: Hachette.

Mannheim, K (1952) *Essays on the Sociology of Knowledge*. London: Routledge & Kegan Paul.

Maslow, A H (1943) A Theory of Human Motivation. *Psychological Review*, 50(4): 370–96.

Moore, L (2012) Millenials in Social Work Field Education. *Field Educator Practice Digest*, 2(2): 1–5.

Oblinger, D (2003) Boomers, Gen-Xers and Millennials. Understanding the New Students. *Educause Review*, 38(4): 37–39.

Perram, A, Hills, C, Johnston, C, MacDonald-Wicks, L, Surjan, Y, James, D and Warren-Forward, H (2016) Characteristics of an Ideal Practice Educator: Perspectives from Undergraduate Students in Diagnostic Radiography, Nuclear Medicine, Nutrition and Dietetics, Occupational Therapy, Physiotherapy and Radiation Therapy. *Radiography*, 22(4): 295–305. doi:10.1016/j.radi.2016.04.007

Prendergast, D (2009) Generational Theory and Home Economics: Future Proofing the Profession. *Family and Consumer Sciences Research Journal*, 37(4): 504–52.

Prensky, M (2001) Digital Natives, Digital Immigrants. *On the Horizon*, 9(5): 1–6.

Rickes, P C (2009) Make Way for the Millennials! How Today's Students' Are Shaping Higher Education. *Planning for Higher Education*, 37(2): 7–17.

Shaw, S and Fairhurst, D (2008) Engaging a New Generation of Graduates. *Education and Training*, 50(5): 366–78. doi: 10.1108/00400910810889057

Sternberg, J (2012) 'It's the End of the University as We Know It (and I Feel Fine)': The Generation Y Student in Higher Education Discourse. *Higher Education Research & Development*, 31(4): 571–83. doi:10/1080/07294360.2011.559193

Tulgan, B and Martin, C A (2001) *Managing Generation Y: Global Citizens Born in the Late Seventies and Early Eighties*. Amherst, MA: HRD Press.

Twenge, J M (2006) *Generation Me*. New York: Free Press.

Twenge, J M (2009) Generational Changes and Their Impact in the Classroom: Teaching Generation Me. *Medical Education*, 43: 398–405.

Twenge, J M and Campbell, W K (2008) Increases in Positive Self-Views Among High School Students: Birth Cohort Changes in Anticipated Performance, Self-Satisfaction, Self-Liking, and Self-Competence. *Psychological Science*, 19: 1082–86.

Twenge, J M and Foster, D F (2010) Birth Cohort Increases in Narcissistic Personality Traits among American College Students, 1982–2009. *Social Psychological and Personality Science*, 1(1): 99–106. doi:10.1177/1948550609355719

Willingham, D T (2010) Have Technology and Multitasking Rewired How Students Learn? *American Educator*, Summer, 23–8.

| **Capabilities and standards: Introducing the Problem-Based Capability Model (PBC) – a holistic tool for teaching and assessing social work practice**

Jackie Plenty and Heidi Dix

Introduction

Social work practice, education and training have long been subject to review, revision and development, which reflects the complexities that surround social work practice in an ever-changing society. Social work students therefore need to undergo intensive training, developing their knowledge, skills and value base in both the academic arena and in practice placements, with a commitment to ongoing continued professional development throughout their careers. Alongside this, the development of the practice educator role has evolved to accommodate and reflect the increasing demands placed on social work students in the face of the dynamic and inconstant socio-economic political arena.

This chapter will explore the Professional Capabilities Framework (PCF) ('refreshed' by the British Association of Social Work (BASW) in 2018) and the Standards of Proficiency for Social Work (SOPs) (HCPC, 2017) as well as considering the role of Problem-Based Learning (Barell, 2007) in the development of social work students. It will also discuss the Signs of Safety framework (Turnell, 2012) that is currently being adopted both nationally and internationally in social work practice. We will introduce the Problem-Based Capability Model (PBC), a holistic tool that can be used by practice educators, supervisors and tutors for the teaching, learning, assessment and supervision of social work students, and which enables the student and supervisor/assessor to work progressively and holistically towards meeting the PCF (BASW 2018). We will then demonstrate how the two contemporary approaches to practice and education mentioned above can fit with the PBC holistic tool to aid student learning.

The Professional Capabilities Framework (PCF) and Standards of Proficiency for Social Work (SOPs)

In essence, the PCF and SOPs take students on a journey from initial training which continues through to their qualifying and post-qualifying experience as part of continued professional development. The 'staged' approach of the PCF assesses students initially in terms of 'Readiness for Practice', following which their capabilities are assessed at 'the end of the first placement' and 'end of final placement', leading on to the Assessed and Supported Year in Employment (ASYE) (Skills for Care, 2015, BASW 2018). Durkin and Shergill (2000, p 171) state that practice competence is concerned with what people can do, rather than what they know; thus, if competence is concerned with 'doing' then it must be related to context or subject, allowing the practice educator to fully evaluate a student's performance (Plenty and Gower, 2013, p 3).

The PCF is set up under nine domains (Figure 2.1) that require the practice educator and student to work together holistically to assess the student's performance.

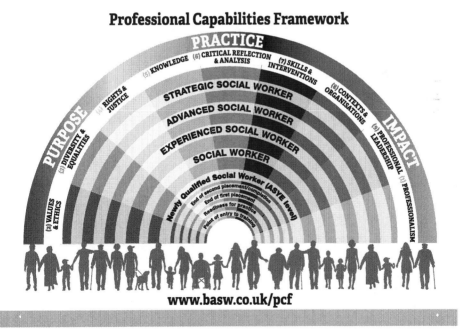

Figure 2.1 Social Work Professional Capabilities Framework

(BASW, 2018)

The PCF depicted in Figure 2.1 names the nine domains at the top of the coloured segments of the outer semi-circle. The innermost semi-circle is where social work students embark on their journey from 'entry to qualifying' programmes through to 'end of last placement'. The Framework then moves into the Assessed and Supported Year in Employment through to the different levels of responsibility incorporating practice, education and management.

In tandem with this, the Health and Care Professions Council, the current regulatory body for social work, set out a list of 15 Standards of Proficiency for Social Work (SOPs) that are linked to the PCF (see HCPC, 2017).

Task 2.1

To familiarise yourself with the PCF, visit the BASW website. Find where your student is currently in relation to their training and development and click on the segments to learn more about the domains within the framework. From this same area of the website you can also download tables that list the domains and their descriptions for the different levels of social work training and practice.

Visit the Health and Care Professions Council website and familiarise yourself with the Standards of Proficiency for Social Workers.

For both students and new practice educators, the PCF (BASW, 2018) and SOPs (HCPC, 2017) frameworks can feel overwhelming when first introduced. Guidance and support is often required from social work programme providers to enable the integration of the Frameworks into academic teaching and learning and across the practice placement experience.

Although the PCF (BASW 2018) is intended to be used holistically, with the domains overlapping and coming together through academic teaching and learning and practice placement experience, there is still a tendency for students and practice educators to use the PCF and SOPs tables as a checklist as the placement progresses. In response to this, some Higher Education Institutes (HEIs) have been developing more creative ways that promote a move away from a 'tick-box' approach towards a more holistic form of assessement.

It is from this basis that the Problem-Based Capability Model (PBC) was developed. Using this model enables students and practice educators to work together to present and gather evidence holistically, incorporating the PCF, while at the same time utilising contemporary models of adult learning, ie Problem-Based Learning (Barell,

2007) and Signs of Safety (Turnell, 2012). Before we move into exploring how to use the PBC model, we will briefly explore some of the principles within the Problem-Based Learning and Signs of Safety approach which underpin the model.

Problem-Based Learning

Problem-Based Learning (PBL) can be defined as: '*An inquiry process that resolves questions, curiosities, doubts and uncertainties about complex phenomena in life and in this case in Social Work Practice. It is a way of challenging students to become deeply involved in a quest for knowledge*' (Barell, 2007, p 3). Although PBL was first developed during the 1960s in the medical arena, the approach has been adopted by some social work training programmes to prepare students for acquiring the knowledge, skills and values needed to work effectively as social work practitioners. Perkins (1992) explains that it teaches students to process information at a higher level, allowing them to adopt inquiring strategies, alongside reflection. Marzano (2003) suggests that it requires multiple exposure to and complex interactions with knowledge, skills and attitudes in a variety of contexts for students to fully engage and absorb information. SCANS (1991) links PBL to decision-making, creative thinking and critical reasoning skills and Barell (2007) explains that high levels of intellectual challenge can be very motivational for students, giving them an opportunity to think and make choices with their peers. Some social work programmes may not directly incorporate this way of learning into their programmes but will certainly indirectly use the principles of a PBL approach in areas of the teaching and learning experience.

Essentially, the PBL model allows groups of students to work holistically towards achieving a goal, enabling them to 'work together' and build themselves into a fully functioning autonomous group that can support each other throughout their training and development. At the same time, they are learning how to 'problem-solve' with service users, each other and their tutors. The tutor will usually take on the role of facilitator, that is, supporting the students to reach their goal through prompting and re-directing, rather than 'teaching' and providing answers. Students take on the responsibilities and roles of chair-person and scribe in their groups, learning how to develop a group agreement, at the same time as ensuring that all the teaching and learning that takes place is recorded and disseminated within the group.

Students will usually be given a case study and will initially 'mind-map' this, working out what they already know, noting down questions and ideas around areas they may need to research. They share out the research tasks and, in smaller groups, begin to inquire about areas within the case about which more knowledge needs to be gained.

This can include reading texts/articles, attending lectures that feature the case study, visiting agencies and investigating resources in the community, and interviewing a range of professional consultants and service users. Once students have worked together in small groups to gather their research, they present their findings to the wider group, which allows the group as a whole to build on the knowledge they previously had. Finally, they will develop a plan that considers key elements within the case, using a 'who, when, why, how' model to plan their assessment and intervention with the service users identified in the case. They are given space to form a hypothesis and present this and suggested ways forward to their tutor and to review and reflect on the PBL process they have journeyed through. It is not difficult to envisage the wide variety of knowledge and skills that students will develop throughout this process, alongside having to explore their own value base, while working out their contribution to, and place within, the group in terms of exploring how they are perceived by their peers and how they identify areas for their own self-development. It also mirrors multi-agency working in the sense that not all groups will naturally 'get on', and will disagree and in many cases will face barriers around 'working together' with others.

The experience can therefore allow students to reflect upon and devise responses and approaches to a variety of complex situations, learning about themselves and the impact they can have on others, at the same time as developing a growing knowledge and skill base around social work practice. It is important that students and practice educators work together to transfer the principles embedded in the PBL approach into real case scenarios and experiences in the social work practice placement arena.

Task 2.2

Think about how you can use the principles embedded in the PBL approach in your student's social work practice placement. For example, students can bring a case they are working on into supervision and, drawing on the principles of the PBL approach (Barell, 2007), explore what they think they already know. You can then together devise a list of research tasks for the student to undertake to further develop their knowledge. In the next session the student can present their findings and use this information to begin to develop a hypothesis which they could use to co-produce a plan with users of services and their families and networks. The law, policy, values and theoretical models that underpin the plan, all of which are linked to the PCF, can also be considered. Students and practice educators can then evaluate and reflect upon the evidence presented and the experience.

Signs of Safety approach

The Signs of Safety approach was developed in the 1990s in Western Australia and adopted by the Child Protection Department of the government of Western Australia in 2008. Since then it has been adopted nationally and internationally, extending beyond work with children and families to work with vulnerable adults (Department of Health, 2017). In essence, it is a strengths-orientated approach which seeks to create a more constructive culture that allows professionals and service users to engage more effectively together. It works on the principles of enhancing 'working relationships' and adopts Munro's maxim (Munro, 2011) around thinking critically and fostering a stance of inquiry, drawing on the expressed wisdom and knowledge of those involved in the process as experts on themselves.

At its simplest, the framework utilises elements of appreciative inquiry and a solution-focused approach (De Shazer and Dolan, 2007) to explore areas of both risk and strength across four key domains, framed as questions, as follows:

» What are you worried about?

» What's working well?

» What needs to happen?

» Scaling question

(Turnell et al, 2017)

Underpinning this approach is the use of straightforward language that avoids judgement-laden terms and which promotes the skilful use of authority with an underlying assumption that assessment is a 'work in progress' rather than a definitive 'set piece' (Turnell, 2012, pp 30–1). Although Signs of Safety provides an assessment framework and easy-to-use working tools, it comprehensively addresses the disjunction that can exist between a problem and a solution-focused approach. Turnell (2012, p 28) explains it as *'a form of simplicity that synthesises considerable complexity'*. Central to the approach is the idea that the more professionals honour the lived experiences of the people they are working with, the more likely they are to listen and are therefore better able to utilise the legitimate authority inherent within their role to better effect. It also moves professionals away from the idea that they are responsible for solving the problems that exist within the family and instead requires them to be transparent and to share their concerns. The skilful use of questioning and inquiry encourages families and their support network to take ownership and devise their own solutions to promote safety and well-being (Turnell, 2013).

With the growing and widespread use of the Signs of Safety approach, students may find themselves placed in agencies that have adopted this model of practice and are likely to be given the opportunity to undertake in-depth training to become familiar with the framework. Likewise, social work training providers are incorporating such training into their own programmes so that students can benefit from the principles and tools used with the approach as soon as they enter their practice placement.

Task 2.3 A joint one for students and practice educators to complete

Draw a table with the headings below:

What are you worried about?	What's working well?	What needs to happen?

Think of a case your student is working on or think about your experience of supervision. Write down your thoughts under the above headings and encourage your student to do the same. When you have some reflections under each of the headings, pull together what you have written in the first two columns into a short paragraph, avoiding the use of jargon. Then do the same for your notes in the final column and share both paragraphs in your next supervision session. Using this approach can open up a dialogue which is honest and transparent and fosters a stance of inquiry which can help promote a positive working relationship.

It has not been the intention of this brief overview of the above approaches used in professional social work practice and the teaching and learning of students to minimise their use and complexity, but rather to provide an opportunity to explore some of the principles in simplified 'bite-size' chunks. Social work education requires all students to undertake research and we encourage practice educators and academics also to become curious about these approaches and to undertake their own reading and research to better understand these frameworks.

Thus, having explored the Professional Capabilities Framework (BASW, 2018) and looked at the Standards of Proficiency for Social Work (HCPC, 2017), alongside some of the principles that underpin a Problem-Based Learning and Signs of Safety approach, we can look at how we can bring these together through the use of a practical tool that can aid the holistic gathering of evidence.

Using the Problem-Based Capability Model

The Problem-Based Capability (PBC) Model (Figure 2.2) largely came about as a result of students and practice educators finding it difficult to navigate their way around the PCF (Plenty and Gower, 2013), resulting in them having a tendency to go through the list of descriptors set against the domains in the PCF tables in a 'tick-box' fashion. Its purpose is to encourage creativity in case work, drawing on different approaches that aid the development of knowledge and skills alongside the exploration of personal and professional values. Although in terms of process it is more specifically linked to some of the principles within both PBL (Barell, 2007) and Signs of Safety (Turnell, 2012), using this model also allows the integration of a wide body of law, policy, research and other theories and models to be considered.

The model can be used by students to prepare them for presenting information and discussing case work in supervision with their practice educators. The PBC model uses the principles within PBL and thus it encourages inquiry and case exploration, research and action planning (Barell, 2007). It also embraces the mapping process used within the Signs of Safety approach (Turnell, 2012) which asks us to consider what we are worried about, what is going well and what needs to happen. Down the left-hand-side of the table are the nine domains of the PCF (BASW, 2015). The PBC model groups the nine domains into three sections in order to allow students to focus on key areas during the periods between their supervision sessions with practice educators or between teaching and learning sessions on social work programmes.

The boxes use the detail that is set out in the PCF domain descriptors (BASW, 2018) using key phrases and words to create questions and tasks for students to research and explore in readiness for critically examining, discussing and reflecting on the findings in supervision or teaching and learning environments. For example, under the first column in the first box, students can begin inquiring and exploring areas within the case, considering aspects of the case that may be of concern and others where there is evidence that things are working well. This will be linked to an exploration of the first three domains of the PCF, namely, professionalism, values and ethics, and diversity. Students can then go on to identify what they know and what they need to know and will begin to plan how to develop relationships with the service user, families and other professionals in order to gain this information. Any gaps in knowledge can therefore be identified and a set of tasks to complete and be discussed and agreed. Students then move onto the final column where the focus is on producing the next steps in relation to the case. The detail in the boxes helps to focus thinking on key areas within the PCF (BASW, 2018) that are directly linked to practice. The model is flexible enough to either work through all three sections (nine domains) under the first column of inquiry and case exploration, using later supervision sessions to present research and findings, or all three columns can be considered, focusing initially on the first three domains within the PCF (BASW, 2018) and then repeating this process for the other domains (in section 2 and 3) in later sessions.

The model can be used with students across three or more supervision sessions and can be completed in a six to eight-week period depending on the frequency of supervision. It allows both practice educator and student to explore an identified and agreed case in which the student is involved, providing clear tasks that need to be undertaken that will ultimately demonstrate how the domains within the PCF (BASW, 2018) have been evidenced. This model can be repeated throughout the placement, giving supervision a focus while ensuring that students are proactive both inside and outside of supervision. As noted previously, students can make use of this model by themselves, as it enables them to think about areas they may wish to discuss in supervision. The model can also be used on social work training programmes to prepare students for moving through the different levels of the PCF across the two/three years of training and into the Assessed and Supported Year in Employment (Skills for Care, 2012).

As students work their way through the tasks set out in the boxes, they will have an opportunity to bring in relevant research, law and policy, and consider how they can integrate a wide range of theories and models, at the same time as developing and evidencing communication and interviewing skills. They will need to demonstrate their understanding of values and ethics, and their ability to keep the family/service user at the heart of the assessment and intervention processes, alongside considering multi-agency working, networking, accessing resources, and organisational structure and processes. The student will also have the opportunity to demonstrate their ability to record and present information and to manage and organise their workload, appreciating the importance of professional responsibility and an understanding of the importance of co-production with service users, as well as contributing to and learning from organisational and teamwork processes.

Essentially, the PBC model reduces the lengthy PCF tables (with descriptors) to one page, without losing key elements of the descriptors set against each of the nine domains within the PCF (BASW, 2018). Students, practice educators and tutors are encouraged to refer to the full PCF for clarification when needed. Ultimately, however, if students work through all areas of the PBC model, at the end of the process they will automatically have engaged with the capabilities through practice and discussion, allowing them to overlap and flow through the work holistically, without having to resort to 'ticking off' the PCF descriptors and thus avoiding exploring the capabilities 'in isolation'.

		⇨		
⇩		**Problem-Based Learning Sequences (Barell, 2007)**		
P	**PCF capabilities (BASW, 2015)**	**Inquiry and case exploration What are we worried about? What's working well?**	**Research and presentation What are we worried about? What's working well?**	**Action planning and evaluation** ⇨ **What needs to happen? Signs of Safety (Turnell, 2012)**
1 **2** **3**	**Section 1** **Professionalism** **Values and Ethics** **Diversity**	Discuss a case or situation you are working with, identifying key aspects of your role drawing on aspects of social policy and law. Think about ethical principles that might arise. Have you considered identity factors such as ethnicity, culture, gender and sexuality? Have you considered the economic status and life experiences impacting on the service user(s)? How will you manage the power inherent within your social work role?	Identify gaps in your knowledge and undertake research and use supervision to present new information. Look at the conduct and ethics for student social workers and consider potentially conflicting ethical dilemmas that might arise through the case. Think about areas where discrimination and conflict may arise and how you will uphold anti-oppressive and anti-discriminatory practice?	Develop a hypothesis and/or plan of action, demonstrating your ability to manage your time and workload. Evaluate your hypothesis/plan and think about how you are making use of guidance and support in supervision. Consider professional and personal boundaries. How will you promote rights to autonomy and self-determination, and effective working in partnership in the face of potential power imbalances? How might your personal values conflict with professional values?

Figure 2.2 Problem-Based Capability Model (PBC): A holistic tool for practice educators and social work students.

4	Section 2	In what ways does poverty and social exclusion potentially impact on the case and how will you promote social justice and inclusion? Have you considered human growth and development across the lifespan in relation to the case? What is the impact of psychological, socio-economic, environmental and physiological factors on people's lives?	Research how law and policy can protect service users in this area and consider how it can be constraining and effect service users' rights. Present information on your understanding of Human Rights and promoting equality and social inclusion.	Consider as part of your hypothesis/ plan how you will use skills of advocacy, demonstrating knowledge of independent advocacy services. How will you consider potential safeguarding issues and potential risk factors relating to the case? Link this to your thoughts in relation to effective assessment and intervention strategies
5	**Rights, Justice and Economic Well-being**			
6				
7	**Knowledge**			
8	**Critical**			
9	**Reflection and Analysis**		Consider the impact of attachment, separation, loss, change and resilience in the life of the service user(s). Explain how you have inquired about areas of the case and how you have assessed the reliability and validity of the research sources and resources you have accessed. Present your understanding of how you have critically reflected on and assessed the usefulness or not of the theories you have used to underpin your decision-making. Think about how you might have applied imagination and creativity in relation to your practice.	Evaluate the case using a strengths perspective, consider areas of resilience and areas of vulnerability and link this to theories you have been using to underpin your practice. Consider the strengths and weaknesses within the theories. In what ways will other professionals be involved? Critically consider the issues that can arise through the process of working together with other professionals and the impact this can have on service users. Use your reflective log to demonstrate how you have considered empowerment and have evaluated and have taken into account the expertise of others.
		Demonstrate your ability to make evidence-informed judgements and to critically reflect on and assess decision-making processes and the impact this can have on service users.		
		How have you kept service users at the heart of the inquiry, assessment and intervention?		

	Section 3 **Intervention and Skills** **Contexts and Organisations** **Professional Leadership**	How have you demonstrated your ability to communicate information, advice, and professional opinion so as to advocate, influence and persuade in respect of the case? How you will be accountable as the social worker taking a lead role in the case? How will you make use of the guidance/support you receive from supervisors and the team? How have you contributed to team working?	What have you learned about methods of communication through research you have undertaken? Demonstrate your understanding of verbal, non-verbal and written methods of communication in line with people's ages, comprehension and culture. Present how you have taken a planned and structured approach to assessment and intervention to promote positive change in line with safeguarding and preventing harm. How does this link to local policy and procedure?	In what ways has your hypothesis/ plan considered the availability of community resources, groups and networks to enhance outcomes for the service users? Did you use your authority as a social worker to access service provision? Evaluate your ability to manage timeframes, organise your time and prioritise areas of the case, making links to records and reports. How have you considered the structure of the organisation in terms of the resources made available and processes for accessing those resources? Were there any barriers? Think about the positive and negative aspects of team working and multi-agency working. How have you utilised your lead role with the case you are working on to engage other professionals and service user/ carers? Reflect on your experiences of sharing and supporting the learning and development of others and in turn think of examples where this has been of benefit to you.

The research that the students undertake and the discussion that unfolds in supervision will also provide evidence, both observed and written, that students, practice educators and tutors can utilise in their written records and reports as part of the assessment process. It will also allow both students and practice educators to more clearly identify gaps in teaching, learning and practice that can form the basis of discussion in later supervision sessions, thus ensuring that there is space to focus on those areas that need further development.

The Problem-Based Capability (PBC model is just one way to think about how to capture the capabilities holistically through teaching and learning in the classroom and through the practice learning experience. It is, however, important to remember that the Professional Capabilities Framework (PCF) (BASW, 2018) is also closely linked to the Standards of Proficiency for Social Work (HCPC, 2017) and thus, in working with and evidencing the capabilities, students are also considering the standards. Individual HEIs will have different methods and tools that they have creatively adapted using the PCF to set up teaching and learning aids and assessment tasks.

Follow the guidance in the next task box to begin the process of making use of the PBC model.

Task 2.4

Students: Copy the PBC model in Figure 2.2 and keep a copy of it to refer to as you begin working through the learning opportunities made available to you in your social work placement setting. Follow the tasks at a pace that works for you so that you develop your knowledge, skills and value base at the same time as gathering evidence to present in supervision with your practice educator and which can be used to provide evidence for your practice placement portfolio. It will help you to identify areas in which you need to increase your knowledge, allowing you to take a proactive approach to setting the agenda for supervision.

Practice educators and students: Decide together how you are going to utilise the model through supervision in your placement setting. In the first session, read through the detail in the boxes in the three columns set across section 1 that incorporates the first three domains of the PCF (TCSW, 2012). Plan together how you will mind-map the case, undertake research in areas where more knowledge or information is required, and present the findings and hypothesis and/or action plan. In the second supervision session, read through the next three PCF domains in section 2 and repeat the process above.

Do the same in the final supervision session and together you will have explored the nine domains of the PCF (BASW 2015) at the same time as underpinning this with some of the principles of both PBL (Barell, 2007) and Signs of Safety (Turnell, 2012). Together you can identify gaps in learning and decide what to focus on in future supervision sessions.

Academics/tutors: You may already be part of a social work training programme in which PBL is embedded into teaching and learning or you may indirectly be using the principles of PBL as part of teaching and learning on the programme. Equally you may be incorporating the Signs of Safety approach into lectures and workshops and/or working with partner agencies that have adopted this approach. All programmes will be working with the PCF (BASW, 2018). You can use the PBC model in tutorials or seminars, in the same way as for practice educators and students (above), using simulated cases or real cases that students bring from their social work practice placements.

Conclusion

This chapter has taken you through the Professional Capabilities Framework (BASW, 2018) as well as considering the Standards of Proficiency for Social Work (HCPC, 2017) which are closely mapped to the PCF. Remember it is a requirement for all social work students and qualified practitioners to become familiar with and to practise within the PCF throughout their careers. However, there is always a need to remain open and responsive to change, in order to incorporate changes taking place in social work more widely, for example, the forthcoming move in regulation from the Health and Care Professions Council to the newly created 'Social Work England'.

We also need to give full credit to Barell (2007), who has written extensively about the use of PBL as an inquiry approach to practice and to Turnell (2012), who continues to promote the Signs of Safety framework. Both these approaches provide useful frameworks for social work practice in their own right but we need to remain aware of the need for social workers to draw on a wide body of research, theory and models and to adhere to social work values throughout their training and professional careers.

The PBL model enables students, practice educators and tutors to capture the descriptors that underpin the nine domains within the PCF at the same time as drawing on some of the principles within other models. This enables the development of practice skills and the acquisition of knowledge, as well as providing a platform for the exploration of personal and professional values.

Social work has, throughout its history, demonstrated the ability to respond to change, adapting and reshaping itself to meet the requirements of an ever-changing society and the influence of different political processes. It is for this reason that we need to maintain a position that embraces an open approach to change, having the curiosity to question and the ability to challenge. Being creative and innovative in our practice helps to ensure we maintain our capacity to provide a high-quality student experience and provide positive outcomes for users of services. Of course, this all needs to be achieved within a wider political and economic climate that will undoubtedly continue to influence the future of the profession.

References

Barell, J (2007) *Problem-Based Learning: An Inquiry Approach* (2nd ed). London: Sage.

British Association of Social Workers (BASW) (2018) Refresh of Professional Capabilities for Social Work (documents available on BASW site).

Department of Health (2017) *Strengths-Based Social Work Practice with Adults – Roundtable Report.* London: DfE.

De Shazer, S and Dolan, Y (2007) (eds) *More than Miracles: The State of the Art of Solution-Focused Brief Therapy.* Binghamton, NY: The Haworth Press Inc.

Durkin, C and Shergill, M (2000) A Team Approach to Practice Teaching. *Social Work Education,* 19(2): 165–74.

Health and Care Professions Council (HCPC) (2017) *Standards of Proficiency: Social Workers in England.* London, HCPC. [online] Available at: www.hcpc-uk.org/publications/standards/index.asp?id=569 (accessed 23 June 2018).

Marzano, R (2003) *What Works in Schools: Translating Research into Action* Alexandria, VA: Association for Supervision and Curriculum Development.

Munro, E (2011) *Review of Child Protection, Final Report: A Child-Centred System* London: DfE.

Perkins, D (1992) *Smart Schools.* New York: Basic Books.

Plenty, J and Gower, D (2013) The Reform of Practice Education and Training and Supporting Practice Educators. *Journal of Practice Teaching and Learning,* 12(2): 48–66.

SCANS (1991) *What Work Requires of Schools. A SCANS Report for America 2000* (Executive Summary). Washington, DC: US Department of Labor, Secretary's Commission on Achieving Necessary Skills.

Skills for Care (2015) *Social Work.* [online] Available at: www.skillsforcare.org.uk/Topics/Social-work/Social-work.aspx (accessed 23 June 2018).

Turnell, A (2012) *Signs of Safety: Briefing Paper.* Perth, Australia: Resolutions Consultancy Ltd.

Turnell, A (2013) *Signs of Safety: Safety Planning Workbook.* Perth, Australia. Resolutions Consultancy Ltd.

Turnell, A, Etherington, K and Turnell, P (2017) *Signs of Safety: Safety Planning Workbook* (2nd ed). Perth. Resolutions Consultancy Ltd.

Chapter 3

Supervision within placement: Achieving best practice

Heidi Dix

Introduction

When students first hear that as part of their placement they will receive something called supervision, those who have not experienced this before may feel anxious and unsure what to expect. Similarly, students who have been supervised in a previous role may have some concerns based on their previous experiences. This chapter provides you with an insight into the supervision process and it will equip you with the following information:

» What supervision is and why it is necessary.

» Different models of supervision in practice learning.

» An insight into what students can expect from their supervisors and practice educators.

» How to get the most from supervision.

So what is supervision and why is it necessary for students?

Supervision has been an important aspect of social work practice for both qualified workers and students for many years. It is a process which serves a number of purposes, most important of which is ensuring that the interests of service users and carers are prioritised and that service users, practitioners and students are kept safe. There has been a recognition through formal enquiries and reports such as serious case reviews (Lord Laming, 2009; Brandon et al, 2012) and the Munro Review into services to protect children (2011) that employers have a responsibility to provide good-quality reflective supervision to their employees. This is also the case for student social workers who can expect a higher level of supervision than qualified practitioners.

Supervision often conjures up images of supervisors overseeing and inspecting the work of groups or individuals. However, Doel (2010), building on the work of Kadushin (1992), suggests that the supervision of social work students has four related but separate elements which he calls ESMA – education, support, management and assessment. Supervision that consists of these four components offers more than just the overseeing of students' practice while they are in placement. For some students, supervision may be provided by two different people – an on-site supervisor and a practice educator – and the differences between these roles will be explained later in this chapter.

ESMA: The four components of student supervision

Education

An important element that students may expect within supervision is education. This aspect of supervision may involve the practice educator supporting the student's teaching and learning in a number of ways, for example, through formal teaching methods such as the sharing of information, eg looking at legislation and social policy, that is pertinent to the practice area and/or supporting the student to relate theory to a practice context. Students can also expect supervision to include indirect teaching methods such as discussions which promote an analysis of the student's actions with service users and colleagues, which has been termed 'reflection on action' (Schön, 1983). Students will also have opportunities to shadow the practice of others, including that of practice educators, supervisors and other colleagues. This means observing, listening and reflecting on what they have observed. These are valuable learning opportunities which require the student to think about what they have experienced, how they felt, what they noticed and what they missed. Talking about things the student did not even notice provides additional opportunities for the student to develop their skills.

Support

Support is also something that students can expect from their supervision sessions. Undertaking direct work with vulnerable people for the first time can provoke anxieties for some students, even those with substantial experience, and therefore supervision can provide a safe space where reassurance can be offered. Rogers and Horrocks (2010) suggest that adult learners have different needs from those of children and bring to education a range of experiences and values from their childhood which may be both positive and negative. Students often find that it is the relationship that is developed in supervision with the practice educator that enables them to explore previous experiences and consider how these may be affecting their ability to learn.

However, it is important to acknowledge that social work supervision sessions are not counselling sessions and it may be that the practice educator suggests to the student that they access independent counselling (which may be available through the university) if there are unresolved issues that may affect their future social work practice (Doel, 2010).

Management

This aspect of supervision includes ensuring that agency policies and procedures have been adhered to. For example, on-site supervisors or practice educators need to ensure that students are aware of and adhering to the lone worker policy, or that they understand the agency's requirements regarding the recording of work. It can also include detailed case discussions to ensure that both service users and students are protected and that cases are being managed appropriately. Clarifying the level of autonomy students have in placement is also important. What expectations does the agency have of students? What work will they be expected to undertake? How will this be allocated? It is the role of the practice educator and on-site supervisor to clarify the student's role and responsibilities while they are in a placement setting.

Practice educators will also wish to ensure that they are meeting a student's needs in relation to the requirements set by the university, which should be detailed in the form of a Learning Agreement. Doel (2010) describes the social work placement for students as similar to undertaking a journey and this can also be used to describe the supervision process. Students can feel apprehensive about supervision and begin cautiously, but a good practice educator will guide them through these feelings, assisting them to develop skills, knowledge and confidence. As more supervision sessions are undertaken, the practice educator will gradually introduce activities or discussions that become more complex in order to offer deeper learning opportunities as the student's confidence and knowledge increases.

Assessment

A key component of the practice educator's role is to provide a holistic assessment of students using the nine domains of the PCF (as described in Chapter 2). Although the nine domains are the same for all students, the requirements under each of these differ slightly depending on whether the student is undertaking an initial or final placement. This assessment will be informed by direct observations of practice and feedback from other members of the team and also from service users and carers. It will also be informed by discussions in supervision sessions and it is important that students are fully prepared and ready to engage in this process. Practice educators often welcome students directing them to pieces of work they have completed that they feel will meet specific requirements. Engaging in an assessment process that is shared by both student and practice educator can help to minimise the power imbalance that exists in this relationship (Field et al, 2014).

Another key author on supervision is the late Tony Morrison (2005). He suggests that there are four important stakeholders who benefit from supervision (see Figure 3.1):

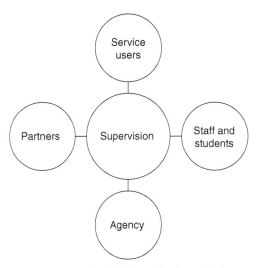

Figure 3.1 Stakeholders who benefit from supervision

(Adapted from Morrison, 2005)

Service users – students who receive effective supervision are more tuned-in to the lived experiences of service users and carers. They become more aware of power issues and are able to provide intervention to users of a service that seeks to be non-oppressive.
Staff and students are clear about the role and responsibilities they have within the agency they are working within as these can be clearly identified in supervision where boundaries can be clarified. Students are able to explore risk issues with their practice educators and as a consequence are able to develop their ability to provide creative interventions that are informed by evidence and practice wisdom.
The **agency** can be confident students are echoing consistent practice that is required within the service and are aware of and adhering to the policies and procedures of the organisation.

Partners – through supervision, an understanding of differing professional roles and organisational cultures that promote multi-agency working can be explored. This in turn can lead to effective communication between various workers from differing disciplines that are involved in the case in order to achieve positive outcomes for service users and carers.

In addition to the above, practice educators benefit in a variety of ways from providing effective supervision to students. Students often experience supervision as a one-way process where they are learning from experienced social workers, but in reality supervision is a shared process which can be of mutual benefit to both parties. Practice educators often comment that providing supervision to students helps to consolidate some of their own learning as they need to discuss the application of theory to practice or revisit their own beliefs and values. Students are often in a position to share their contemporary knowledge of social policy and legislation, as well as introducing new theories and models of social work practice to practice educators who actively welcome this knowledge exchange.

Different types of supervision you can expect on placement

What is the difference between an on-site supervisor and a practice educator?

A practice educator will be a registered social worker who has, or is planning to undertake, a post-qualifying qualification to enable them to provide supervision to social work students and to formally assess that a student has met the necessary requirements specified by the current regulator. An on-site supervisor, often referred to as a practice supervisor, could also be a qualified social worker, but may not have undertaken the necessary qualifications to operate as a practice educator. Alternatively, on-site supervisors may not have a formal social work qualification and may be experienced practitioners or managers in the agency. The latter is often the case in third-sector organisations such as charities and social enterprises where the on-site supervisor may hold other qualifications. For final placements a practice educator must hold the second level of the Practice Educator Professional Standards (see Chapter 2).

Students may find that they have a practice educator who is based within the agency and from whom they will receive weekly supervision. However, in other placements the practice educator is not based within the agency and an on-site practice supervisor will be appointed to provide day-to-day support and guidance. Students who have an on-site practice supervisor in addition to their practice educator may find that supervision will be given on alternate weeks by the practice educator and the on-site practice supervisor. The nature and content of supervision provided within these roles is slightly different. For example, supervision with an on-site practice supervisor could focus on the direct work the student is undertaking and have more of a managerial focus, for example, ensuring that the student is working within the agency's eligibility criteria. However, supervision with a practice educator may have more of an educational and reflective focus, supporting the student to apply the knowledge they are learning in university and their self-directed learning to the work they are undertaking in placement.

Below are some comments from students in relation to the advantages and disadvantages of off-site and on-site models of practice education which I have heard over the years. Of course, these are generalisations and will not apply in all situations, but it is worth noting the strengths and limitations of both models. However, the most important thing is that the practice educator and practice supervisor work together to meet the learning needs of each individual student.

Advantages of having an off-site practice educator and on-site supervisor	Disadvantages of having an off-site practice educator and on-site supervisor
'If practice educators are not directly working within the agency they can provide greater objectivity and support students to question agency policy, procedures and practice.'	'Practice educators may not have direct practice experience in the area of social work that students are placed in.'
'Off-site practice educators often bring experience from other areas of social work, enabling students to compare and contrast their placement with other aspects of social work practice.'	'Off-site practice educators are often not available outside scheduled supervision times.'
'Off-site practice educators, particularly those who work independently, will often support a number of students and will often provide group supervision which can be beneficial.'	'Contact with practice educators will be limited, particularly within the 70-day placement.'

Advantages of having an off-site practice educator and on-site supervisor	Disadvantages of having an off-site practice educator and on-site supervisor
'Practice educators will have direct practice experience of the work required within the agency.'	'Students can learn from different approaches and styles, eg "two heads are better than one."'
'They are often available for both formal and informal supervision,'	'Practice educators can be immersed in the culture of the agency and could be adverse to the student asking questions that demonstrate critical reflection.'
'Supervision will be offered on a weekly basis with the same person.'	'Students will need to ensure there are opportunities to shadow other colleagues, not just their on-site practice educator.'

The majority of supervision students receive will be on a one-to-one basis, although there may be occasions when group supervision is used. Students often find this helpful as it enables them to share learning with other students in a practice setting and provides another form of support (Doel, 2010). However, one-to-one sessions are critically important in enabling a student to focus clearly and in depth on issues specific to their individual learning needs, particularly if a student has additional learning needs (see Chapter 8). There are also different expectations of students in their first and final placements as they build on the capabilities demonstrated in the first placement. Although students will still be offered guidance and support in their final placement, they should be given more autonomy as their confidence and ability increases. Students often find that their learning needs change as their confidence increases and consequently require different things from supervision. For example, in early supervision sessions, students may require support to develop their self-belief. However, as students develop in confidence, they may require less of this type of support and supervision could focus more on developing critical thinking skills.

An insight into what students can expect from their supervisors and practice educators

As adult learners, Rogers and Horrocks (2010) suggest that although we will have similar characteristics we also have differing needs depending on a range of factors. These include issues of diversity such as gender, ethnicity and class as well as the level of experience, skills and knowledge that students bring to the programme. Depending on our personality types (Rogers and Horrocks, 2010), the attachment experiences we have received in childhood (Howe et al, 1999) and whether we are operating from a secure base (Bowlby, 1973), we may require more or less support in particular areas of development. Therefore, as part of supervision sessions, students can expect their practice educators to 'tune in' (Taylor and Devine, 1993) to their needs to assist them to identify previous skills and experience in order to assist them appropriately. Research conducted with social work students by Lefevre (2005) suggested that student learning is enhanced when students feel listened to and respected by practice educators; therefore, developing a professional relationship to facilitate effective supervision is helpful to both parties. It is important that each party understands what is expected of the other and this needs to be clarified if there is any confusion.

There are many ways that we learn and take in information. Many of us prefer to have information presented to us visually, some of us find if we hear things we retain them better, others prefer to see things written down, and some of us learn best if we can move around and utilise our senses (Fleming, 1995). For some of us, experiencing something and thinking about it afterwards is the best way that we learn (Kolb, 1984). There are a number of questionnaires that are available to help us understand our learning styles (Honey and Mumford, 1992; Fleming and Baume, 2006) and it may be helpful for students to complete one of these and share the results with their practice educator to enable them to tailor their support to help maximise the student's learning. Although we often have a preferred way of learning, it is important that we have the ability to be receptive to new ways of understanding, because as practitioners we will often work with service users who will have a different way of learning to ourselves. We may need to present information to service users in a way that best meets their needs; practice educators may model this by encouraging students to be flexible and to begin to adopt new ways of receiving and processing information.

Organisations have different policies in relation to the amount of supervision to which employees are entitled. Students may find themselves placed in organisations where supervision is not something that is routinely offered to employees or volunteers. However, qualified social workers employed by a local authority are entitled to regular and consistent supervision (LGA, 2014). As social work students, the frequency of supervision will be determined by the university and negotiated with the placement provider at a Learning Agreement Meeting. In addition to formal supervision sessions, students should be able to 'check out' any questions they have in between sessions by utilising the experience and knowledge of other practitioners within the organisation. If students believe they are not getting the length and quality of the supervision they are entitled to as a social work student, they should be encouraged to inform their university tutor who may need to revisit this with the placement provider or practice educator as part of the Learning Agreement.

Within the first supervision session, the practice educator will complete a supervision agreement. This agreement contains practical details such as where the sessions will take place (the venue, the length of the sessions, how they will be recorded etc). It may also give general details as to what is expected from both the student and the practice educator. An example of a supervision agreement can be seen below.

Supervision agreement

Name of practice educator: Denise Brown

Name of social work student: Leticia O'Connor

Name of on-site practice supervisor: Chris Marston

This supervision agreement serves as a reminder of the professional responsibilities we have towards each other.

Arrangements: Supervision with Denise will take place on a fortnightly basis for approximately 1 hr 30 minutes. The venue will be at Leticia's placement, the Quay side building, in a private room and Leticia will be responsible for booking the room. Interruptions will be kept to a minimum and mobile phones placed on silent.

Priority will be given to supervision sessions and attempts will be made to prevent them being cancelled. However, if this is unavoidable we will give each other reasonable notice and the session will be re-arranged as soon as possible.

Recording: Denise and Leticia will take it in turns to take notes from supervision. These will be signed by both people and copies provided to each of us from the session. Some copies of supervision notes are required to be submitted in Leticia's portfolio and she can identify which notes she wishes to include.

Content: The contents of the agenda for each session will be shared and Leticia is expected to come to supervision with items to discuss and prepared to undertake some reflection on practice, feelings and values on work undertaken. Supervision will also provide a forum for the exchange of knowledge, a review of the PCF and student assessment.

Expectations of supervision

Leticia (student) – What I want from supervision is a chance to talk about my work with service users without feeling that I have to get it right all the time. I would also like some help with relating the theory I am learning in university to the work I am doing on placement.

Denise (practice educator) – I will provide a non-judgemental environment in supervision where we are able to explore and learn from your practice experiences. I will share my professional knowledge to support you to meet the requirements specified by the university. Within supervision sessions we will also need to review the tasks you and I are undertaking and set timescales for the completion of these.

Disagreement: Any differences will be discussed in supervision in the first instance. If this is not able to resolve the issue(s) then the university's procedures will be followed as specified in the handbook.

Signed: **Date:**

Signed: **Date:**

Within supervision sessions, the practice educator will often share their knowledge and practice experience with the student in order to assist them in their learning. There is also an expectation that students will engage in self-directed learning and may be given tasks by the practice educator to complete and bring to the next session. Examples of tasks may include finding the community resources that are available in the area, researching a particular theory that is relevant to the practice setting, or writing a reflective log to be shared in a future session (see the example in the box below).

Case example 3.1

Mark is a social work student placed in a Youth Offending Service. He has a twin brother, Paul, who is a serving police officer. During a supervision session Mark informed Loretta, his practice educator, that Paul often uses derogatory language when he refers to young people in contact with the criminal justice system. After discussing this further with Mark, Loretta asked him to write a piece of reflection, which he was to bring to their next supervision session, exploring how Mark was managing the views expressed by his brother and whether they were in conflict with Mark's personal values, social work values and the values of the Youth Offending Team he was placed in. Mark brought his reflections to his next supervision session and Loretta discussed this with him. She then broadened out the discussion to consider the differences between organisational cultures and how these can impact on service users.

At the start of each session, students can expect their practice educator to formulate an agenda of items to be covered within the session and it is important that students contribute to this list any items they wish to be included. Examples of topics included as part of a shared agenda are as follows:

» case management discussions;

» reflective discussions;

» exploration of personal, professional and social work values and the identification of any conflicts that occur between these;

» anti-discriminatory, anti-oppressive and anti-racist practice;

» application of theory to practice;

» any other business.

Some practice educators may have some or all of the above as standard agenda items, whereas others may cover different issues in supervision as they arise. The important thing is that both parties engage fully in the process. Notes or minutes should be taken at each supervision to record accurately the content of each session. Many practice educators will share this task with students, alternating from session to session. If the practice educator gives the student full responsibility for recording the session, it may be useful for the practice educator to also take notes or minutes at one of the initial sessions in order to demonstrate good note/minute-taking practice and for the student to gain an understanding of the expectations required. The written recording from each session will need to be signed and agreed by both parties.

Getting the most from supervision

The necessity of understanding our thoughts, feelings and emotions – ie 'the use of self' in social work practice is well documented (Ruch et al, 2010; Ruch, 2012; Megele, 2015). Linked to this is the importance for social workers to be emotionally intelligent in order to work effectively with colleagues, other professionals, service users and carers (Howe, 2008).

Goleman (1998) suggested that there five characteristics of an emotionally intelligent person (see table below, based on Morrison, 2012). These characteristics are important in facilitating effective social work practice, but they are equally important for us to participate effectively in supervision sessions. Using emotional intelligence to 'tune in' (Taylor and Devine, 1993) to the practice educator enables students to develop a positive relationship with him/her. 'Tuning in' will not only assist students to meet their needs outlined in supervision and learning agreements but will also enable them to assess and develop an awareness of their own emotional intelligence.

1.	**Self-awareness**	Having knowledge of ourselves, our strengths, limitations and emotions.
2.	**Self-regulation**	Our internal world, eg managing our emotions, having a sense of personal responsibility, being able to be flexible and adapt to new situations.
3.	**Motivation**	A commitment to achieving goals (internal or external), being optimistic and able to take the initiative.
4.	**Empathy**	Having an awareness of others' feelings, needs, perceptions and concerns. This can include colleagues, managers, service users, and also the needs of the organisation.
5.	**Social skills**	An ability to communicate effectively to develop effective relationships to influence others; to negotiate and resolve disagreements and to work effectively in a team.

Psychodynamic approaches to social work allow us to explore the role of our unconscious mind on our thoughts, feelings and behaviour. An idea borrowed from a psychodynamic perspective, that of defence mechanisms (Freud, 1949), may be helpful for students to consider in order to get the best from supervision. Defence mechanisms are behaviours that we have developed over time, which we then apply to situations where we feel very anxious and uncomfortable. These can include the following:

» Denial – refusing to accept something that has been highlighted to us.

» Repression – avoiding a difficult experience by forgetting it.

» Regression – behaving at a younger developmental stage than our current one.

(Wilson et al, 2011)

As outlined earlier, a key feature of supervision will be space for reflection, and this could involve discussions regarding the direct observations of the student's work with service users. It is important to recognise how defence mechanisms can affect a student's ability to receive constructive feedback from their supervisors. Below are some tips for giving and receiving feedback which can assist students to maximise their learning.

Rules for giving feedback	Rules for receiving feedback
Be realistic and specific. Feedback on things that can be changed.	Be open, don't attempt to make justifications, listen and be curious about what they are telling you.
Provide specific examples and wherever possible relate them to concrete observable behaviour.	Suspend your defences – this is feedback of what they are seeing/hearing/feeling. Think about the example they have chosen and reflect on their points.
Must make a positive contribution to professional development. Be aware of your own emotional state before giving feedback so that your focus can be on the other person and not yourself.	If you have a strong reaction to the feedback you have received, reflect on why this is, eg is it because you have been told this before? Do you have a strong reaction because it is something you need to learn?

It may be helpful for students to draw a parallel between the relationship they hope to develop with service users and the one practice educators are hoping to develop with their students. While both sets of relationships carry different power imbalances, practice educators will expect students to be an active participant and engage with the supervision process, rather than being a passive recipient. Supervision is not something that should be done *to* someone, but a helpful process undertaken *with* someone!

As well as utilising emotional intelligence (Goleman, 1998), students also need to be aware that communication can be affected by people 'playing games' (Berne, 1964), which they may be unaware they are playing. Therefore, we need to be aware of our own game playing or that of others in order for communication to be effective. In relation to ourselves, the Johari window (Luft and Ingham, 1955) may help us to understand ourselves better. This model suggests that there are parts of ourselves that we choose to show to others and parts that we choose to keep to ourselves. However, there may also be parts of ourselves that we may be unaware of, though well known to other people, ie our 'blind spot'. This can include our attitudes and the way we behave (Luft and Ingham, 1955; see Figure 3.2).

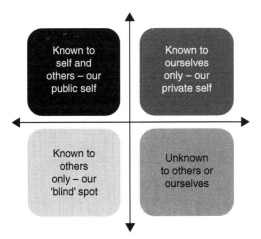

Figure 3.2 Johari window

There is a clear power imbalance between the practice educator and student, and often students can find it difficult to admit they are struggling for a number of reasons, including the fear of not being seen as competent.

Task 3.1

Think about the ways in which you and your student are different. This may include class, sexuality, gender, physical ability, ethnicity and religion. Relate this to your knowledge of power and oppression. Who has more power in each of the differences you have identified? How could these power differentials impact on your relationship? What can be done to minimise any power issues that exist?

Sometimes it may be helpful for students to rehearse supervision sessions in advance with their university tutor, particularly where they are anticipating difficulty or disagreement.

Case example 3.2

Sara is in her first placement and her practice educator is also her on-site supervisor. Sara has read the mid-way report that the practice educator has written about her and feels that it does not adequately reflect the first half of the placement and the skills and knowledge she has learned through her placement experience. There are also some factual inaccuracies contained within the report such as the date of the direct observations she has undertaken. Sara was unsure how to address her thoughts with her practice educator. She asked for a tutorial with her personal tutor at university who suggested different ways Sara could approach the issue with her practice educator. Sara practised saying what she wanted to say with her tutor until she felt confident enough to speak with her practice educator in her next supervision session. Sara reported back to her tutor that the conversation had gone well; she has felt listened to by her practice educator who has amended the report and thanked Sara for speaking with her in a professional manner.

Conclusion

Students suggest that the learning activities that they find most useful to assist them to develop their confidence and prepare them for social work practice include receiving constructive criticism, undertaking observations of their practice educator or other staff, and having opportunities to discuss their feelings and values (Roulston et al, 2014). Supervision can offer a formal space for students to explore fears, anxieties, emotions and feelings in a safe environment. It also offers a forum for learning, ensures that both students and service users are kept safe, and provides opportunities for students to demonstrate their learning to enable the practice educator to make an holistic assessment of their knowledge, skills and ability. However, supervision is very much a partnership and you really will get out what you put in so invest in it wisely!

References

Berne, E (1964) *Games People Play: The Psychology of Human Relationships.* London: Penguin.

Bowlby, J (1973) *Separation: Anxiety and Anger.* London: Hogarth Press.

Brandon, M, Sidebotham, P, Bailey, S, Belderson, P, Hawley, C, Ellis, C and Megson, M (2012) *New Learning from Serious Case Reviews.* Research report DFE-RR226. London: DfE.

Doel, M (2010) *Social Work Placements: A Traveller's Guide.* London: Routledge.

Field, P, Jasper, C and Little, L (2014) *Practice Education in Social Work: Achieving Professional Standards.* Critical Skills for Social Work. Northwich: Critical Publishing Ltd.

Fleming, N D and Baume, D (2006) Learning Styles Again: VARKing up the Right Tree! *Educational Developments*, Issue 7.4: 4–7. [online] Available at: http://vark-learn.com/wp-content/uploads/2014/08/Educational-Developments.pdf (accessed 23 June 2018).

Fleming, N D (1995) I'm Different; Not Dumb. Modes of Presentation (VARK) in the Tertiary Classroom, in Zelmer, A (ed) *Research and Development in Higher Education: Proceedings of the 1995 Annual Conference of the Higher Education and Research Development Society of Australasia* (HERDSA). *HERDSA*, 18: 308–13.

Freud, S (1949) *An Outline of Psychoanalysis.* London: Norton.

Goleman, D (1998) *Working with Emotional Intelligence.* London: Bloomsbury.

Honey, P and Mumford, A (1992) *Manual of Learning Styles* (revised ed). London: Peter Honey.

Howe, D (2008) *The Emotionally Intelligent Social Worker.* Basingstoke: Palgrave Macmillan.

Howe, D, Brandon, M, Hinings, D and Schofield, G (1999) *Attachment Theory, Child Development and Family Support: A Practice and Assessment Model.* Basingstoke: Palgrave Macmillan.

Kadushin, A (1992) *Supervision in Social Work* (3rd ed). New York: Columbia University Press.

Kolb, D A (1984) *Experiential Learning: Experience as the Source of Learning and Development.* Englewood Cliffs, NJ. Prentice Hall.

Laming, W H (2009) *The Protection of Children in England.* London: The Stationary Office.

Lefevre, M (2005) Faciliating Practice Learning and Assessment: The Influence of Relationship. *Social Work Education,* 24(5): 565–83.

Local Government Association (LGA) (2014) *The Standards for Employers of Social Workers in England.* [online] Available at: www.local.gov.uk/documents/10180/6188796/The+Standards++updated+July+01+2014/146988cc-d9c5-4311-97d4-20dfc19397bf (accessed 23 June 2018).

Luft, J and Ingham, H (1955) *The Johari Window: A Graphic Model of Interpersonal Awareness. Proceedings of the western Training Laboratory in Group Development.* Los Angeles: UCLA.

Megele, C (2015) *Psychosocial and Relationship-Based Practice.* Northwich: Critical Publishing Ltd.

Morrison, T (2012) *Staff Supervision in Social Care.* Brighton: Pavilion.

Munro, E (2011) *The Munro Review of Children Protection. Final Report: A Child-Centred System.* London: DfE.

Rogers, A and Horricks, N (2010) *Teaching Adults* (4th ed). Maidenhead: McGraw-Hill Education.

Roulston, A, Cleak, H and Vreugdenhil, A (2014) Final Report on *'Models of Supervision Influencing Student Development in Social Work Practice Learning Opportunities'.* Belfast: Queens University Belfast.

Ruch, G (2012) Where Have All the Feelings Gone? Developing Reflective and Relationship-Based Management in Child-Care Social Work. *British Journal of Social Work,* 42(7): 1315–32.

Ruch, G, Turney, D and Ward, A (2010) *Relationship-Based Social Work: Getting to the Heart of Practice.* London: Jessica Kingsley.

Schön, D A (1983) *The Reflective Practitioner: How Professionals Think in Action.* London: Maurice Temple Smith Ltd.

Taylor, B and Devine, T (1993) *Assessing Needs and Planning Care in Social Work.* Surrey: Ashgate.

The College of Social Work (2012) *Professional Capabilities Framework.* London: The College of Social Work.

The College of Social Work (2013) *Practice Educator Professional Standards for Social Work.* London: The College of Social Work.

Wilson, K, Ruch, G, Lymbery, M and Cooper, A (2011) *Social Work: An Introduction to Contemporary Practice* (2nd ed). Harlow: Pearson.

Chapter 4 | Stories, storytelling and their contribution to learning

Sarah Flanagan

Storytelling is a familiar human practice. Many of us recall listening to stories in our childhood. Stories remembered can range from traditional fairy tales to contemporary narratives delivered by the adult to the child. Reading books and analysing texts are familiar activities within the school environment. There is also some recognition of the contribution that stories can provide to adult learning, particularly for those adults who are engaged in vocational learning where there is a need to make some connection between theory and practice (McDrury and Alterio, 2002; Moon, 2010). This chapter will reflect on the nature of stories and will offer some insights into their characteristics. The value of storytelling, in particular the contribution that stories make to practice learning, will be explored.

The concept of story

When attempting to define stories, an immediate challenge for the writer is one of language. Despite different origins within language (Frid et al, 2000), the words 'story' and 'narrative' are often used interchangeably (Bruner, 1986; Webster and Mertova, 2007; Moon, 2010). Therefore, for the purpose of this chapter the word 'story' will be used. This word is used to encompass case studies, critical incidents, scenarios, narratives from books described as works of fiction and those categorised as factual, for example reflective accounts and official documents.

The fundamental and necessary nature of story is revealed in relevant literature. Moon states that *'Story is everywhere. It is the stuff of our entertainments, our day and night dreams. It is the comfort that we give each other in times of difficulty'* (p 3). The philosopher Ricoeur (1984) emphasises how essential story is to an individual's understanding of their world. Ricoeur uses the concept of time to illustrate his argument. He compares cosmic time and lived time. Cosmic time is fluid and understood through mathematical equations. Lived time is structured and understood through story. Certain tools are used by humans to do this and Ricoeur refers to them as the *'Aporias'* of time (p 8), better known as the past, the present and the future. The past, the present and the future are also common ingredients of story. Ricoeur agrees with fellow philosopher Husserl (1964) that human beings cannot experience the present without an appreciation of what has occurred previously and what may come next. Carr (1991) recognises that Ricoeur's thinking is vulnerable to criticism, that his view of time contrasts with presiding opinion which claims that events occur randomly within time and that providing a sequence to them distorts reality. However, Carr stresses that it is the human *experience* of time to which Ricoeur is referring. Carr's reflection on Ricoeur's work is significant for this chapter as it emphasises how important story can be in the human understanding of an experience within the field of practice learning.

The conceptualisation of story has produced a debate around categorisation. Often stories are perceived as fact or fiction. In his definition of story, Gabriel (2000) describes how there is acknowledgement that stories evolve from fantasy or experience. Moon and Fowler (2008) provide a framework for the categorisation of stories; however, they acknowledge that different categories can overlap. Ricoeur (1990) stresses that, in order to respect those involved in past events and experiencing the impact of history, differentiation between stories claiming to resemble the past and others is necessary. However, Ricoeur also acknowledges that complete separation of different story categories is misleading. He describes how people require imagination to bring a historical account to life and fictitious novels rely on the use of factual events to make them believable.

The categorisation of story does impact on their use within higher education. For example, written reflective accounts of placement are generally perceived as factual narratives of practice that are assessed against prescribed standards (Taylor, 2006). However, these stories like all others are reinterpretations of events (Bruner, 1987; Ricoeur, 1990) and that reinterpretation will be subject to the storyteller's cognitive structure (how they see the world) and how they have understood their experience. Therefore, seeing stories from practice purely as a means of authentically recalling events and demonstrating practice in line with prescribed standards could be underestimating their value.

Task 4.1 Task for students

Reflect on the views of Ricoeur and Bruner. During your day-to-day experience consider how you sequence events to enhance your understanding of them. Do you notice a reference to the past in your current interpretation of the situation and do you consider implications for the future?

Remember – stories are subject to an individual's cognitive structure. This can explain why recollections of events can differ from one individual to another.

You are likely to have a shared experience during placement with a supervisor or fellow student. Share your story of that experience and consider the differences in content and why they may be present.

Bruner offered some insights into the ingredients of a story; this is significant as it suggests that they are recognisable due to their structure. For example, when conversing with your colleagues and peers and a feature of the conversation is a sequence of events that involves the disruption of the familiar, you are likely to be in receipt of a story. Reflect on how often this occurs; it will help illuminate how present story is within your life.

Story and its contribution to learning.

There are a number of theories related to this subject. One perspective particularly relevant to storytelling is social constructivist theory. John Dewey was a philosopher, educationalist and social constructivist. Dewey (1938) believed that knowledge was gained most effectively through experience. However, he believed that experience had to be subject to human interpretation. He claimed that a person's interpretation of experience occurred in light of previous experience and therefore learning was constructed, built over time. Dewey believed that learning was essentially individual in its nature as a new experience would connect differently to each person's varying past. Moon offers insights into this process, stating that a new concept is discarded or connected to our cognitive structure (what we already know, think and feel) through the process of *'assimilation'* (Piaget, 1971 cited in Moon, 2010, p 34). During this process new ideas may simply 'add on' or there may be some adjustment in the new idea or the cognitive structure itself. Adjustment in the cognitive structure is called 'accommodation'. The relevance of story to these ideas about learning is demonstrated firstly in the contribution that story makes to the understanding of the experience; people make links to their past through story. Importantly, people can share their understanding through story. Story can particularly attract a person's attention due to its structure (Bruner, 1986; Moon, 2010). As an individual is more likely to attend to story, there is less chance of a learning opportunity being missed. Significantly, stories introduce new experiences to a person's cognitive structure without the need for their presence at the actual event. Also of significance is the ability of story to capture a person's attention and produce accommodation in an individual's cognitive structure through their emotional content (Chan and Chung, 2004); here, 'accommodation' is stimulated through feeling rather than knowing.

The social constructivist perspective and the beguiling characteristics of story illustrate how in our day-to-day activities and 'lived time' stories contribute to learning.

Contributions include assistance in the understanding of the vital resource for knowledge called experience. Stories create opportunity for experiential learning through others in our social world. This removes the need for an individual to be present at every event that could offer a learning opportunity. Stories help prevent us from missing possible future contributions to our learning and they help us contribute to the learning of others in our ability to share stories. Story sharing also provides the vital opportunity for individuals to express what they know.

Task 4.2 Task for students

During your practice experience you will exchange stories with numerous people, including both staff and people for whom you provide a service. Reflect on the particular stories that capture your attention. Consider why these particular stories have been retained in your memory. Is it the emotional content? Do they relate to your previous experience? Are the stories an add-on reaffirming the knowledge and feelings that you already possess or do you recall a story that has required you to make some adjustment in your cognitive structure? If so, it may be useful to share with your practice supervisor. We know that stories cause significant adjustments in our cognitive structure. People describe how some stories can create a whole new perspective. I have heard the term 'life-changing' used in relation to a person's story.

Story and its relationship with reflective practice

Having considered the contribution that story provides to learning, particularly experiential learning, it would be useful to think about possible links to reflective practice. Both Moon (2010) and McDrury and Alterio (2002) recognise that story makes an important contribution to reflective practice. Atkins and Murphy (1993) state that there is no agreed definition on reflection; however, there is a consensus that reflection includes thinking about experience. McDrury and Alterio state that reflection is *'essentially attending to events that have been brought to the consciousness for re-examination'* (2002, p 106). The value of thinking about previous events in this way is articulated in Schön's work. As described in Chapter 1, Schön (1983) talks about reflection on action, when an individual considers previous events and associated responses. Importantly, Schön viewed this process of reflection as a valuable learning opportunity. He also argued that reflection helped reduce barriers between theory and practice. He stated that the knowledge accrued from effective reflection is in itself a form of informal theory. This informal theory is seen as particularly valuable for professional development and the generation of professional expertise. Often when we consider our actions and their validity, we use knowledge gained from formal training and education to assess our responses. For example, we may think about a relevant theory discussed in a lecture or a piece of legislation covered in an assignment. Kolb (1984) also championed the contribution of experience to learning. Kolb's learning cycle illustrates his perceived requirements for the effective use of experience as a tool for learning. Within the learning cycle, specific reference is made to thinking and utilisation of theory. The work of authors such as Schön and Kolb has led to many vocational courses delivered within higher education promoting reflection (Harrison, 2009), one example being the training of social workers.

Having established that reflection involves thinking about the past, it should also be acknowledged that this process has been formally valued in higher education, particularly within vocational training as a mechanism for reducing gaps between theory and practice. It is pertinent to examine the contribution of story. We know from the work of Ricouer (1984) that story is fundamental in the structuring of our experience; when people think about the past they will sequence it as a story. Importantly as Ricoeur (1984) and Bruner (1987) state, this is not simply a recall of events it is a reinterpretation, which in itself promotes greater understanding. Stories often lend themselves well to the retelling of unsettling events; as Schön (1983) writes, it is often the unsettling, complex events that require reflection on action. Moon (2010) refers to the use of critical incidents in her link between reflection and storytelling. Stories are also thought to fit well with reflective models promoted in higher education, for example Kolb (1984) and Gibbs (1988). The use of past, present and future, which are familiar ingredients of story, is also advocated in the reflective model. Story is thought to stimulate reflection (Flanagan, 2015).

A story's ability to encourage reflection occurs during its sharing. For example, if a student talks about a significant event, their response to the event and the subsequent consequences, another student may think about their own similar experience, how they dealt with it and how their own responses fit with that of their peer. Story trading is acknowledged by McDrury and Alterio (2002). It is also advocated by Moon (2010). Moon believes that sharing stories can enhance reflection as this process offers the opportunity for students to examine alternative perspectives, an action that is thought to improve the depth of reflection. McDrury and Alterio recommend the comparison of written student stories utilising a reflective framework to assess the varying depths of reflection. Alterio (2004) also studied the effects of collaborative journalling as a professional development tool. She concluded that collaborative writing did create multiple perspectives on professional practice and change. Story has been used specifically to analyse decision-making and therefore enhance critical thinking, a process that is explicitly advocated within the reflective models (Kolb, 1984; Gibbs, 1988). Gold and Holman (2001) found that story incorporating decision-making encouraged trainee managers to work cooperatively in their problem-solving. In addition to the exploration of alternative perspectives and opportunity for enhanced analysis of decision-making skills, story also brings an emotional aspect to reflections (McEwan and Egan, 1995; Chan and Chung, 2004; Douglas and Carless, 2009).

The opportunity for students to explore the emotional content of their stories could lead to greater emotional understanding. Goleman (1996) states that an individual's ability to recognise their emotions and the impact of them on their behaviour can lead to better emotional control, which can enhance a person's social interactions and their relationships. Contemporary discussions regarding the desired characteristics of graduates and those in professional roles acknowledge the value of emotional intelligence. There is a view that emotional intelligence can lead to enhanced experiences of employability. Employability is commonly defined as the gaining and retaining of employment that fits with the knowledge and skills of the employee (Trought, 2012). The capacity of stories to provide learners with the opportunity to develop their emotional understanding suggests that stories and their sharing cannot just help in the development of decision-making skills and the management of emotions but facilitate longevity in employment and an enhanced sense of satisfaction. Noddings (1996) provides another insight into how stories may provide resilience, stating that responses evoked or illustrated in stories can help reduce a student's sense of isolation as they recognise similar emotional responses in their peers.

Reflective writing has been used by academic institutions to assess learning and story can provide a valuable opportunity for learners to articulate what they know. As described earlier in the chapter, story categorisation can determine how stories are perceived and used within higher education and also as alluded to previously some blurring between categories of story can occur. Taylor acknowledges this in her study of reflection. She states that it was naive to believe that written extracts were *'what really happened in any given situation'* (2006, p 194). Importantly, Taylor advocates that reflective writing should not for this reason be dismissed as inaccurate and untrue but consists of examples of how students developed their identity and expressed their hopes for practice. Some academics have supported greater use of work formally defined as fiction to stimulate reflection (Hoggan and Cranton, 2015).

Task 4.3 Task for students

Does the idea that story trading stimulates reflection resonate for you? Try to recall examples when you have heard a story and it has reminded you of your own experience, perhaps a similar dilemma. Did the story make you think again about your own response? Did it provide you with an alternative action and make you think or even feel quite powerfully that if a similar event occurred again you would do things differently? Consider a particular story from practice that could be shared with your practice educator/supervisor for the purpose of analysing your decision-making.

The value of reflective writing is well established (Flecknoe, 2001; Bolton, 2006). It is also acknowledged that works of fiction have worth for reflection, particularly when reflecting on emotions. Within your reflective journal and using your imagination, create a formally fictitious entry that communicates how you hoped a particular placement event would be, for example your first day, your meeting with your practice educator. It may then be useful to compare the actual event in your journal, noting the differences and exploring how gaps between hopes and reality could be reduced.

The social impact of story

The literature relating to stories and storytelling informs us that story is a constant presence within people's lives: it assists people in making sense of the world around them. Story is a valuable resource for learning and there is some agreement that story sharing can be extremely useful in helping learners understand alternative perspectives and the emotional elements of story. Given that story is so present and that story sharing occurs and has some value it is important to consider in more detail the social impact of story.

Storytelling requires the involvement of both the storyteller and the listener as they both engage in the reinterpretation of the events and experiences depicted within the story. This process is not a passive one for either participant. The storyteller provides their interpretation, articulating the sequence of events to reveal the plot, and the various characters are introduced. As the listener receives the story they are also interpreting its content, they imagine the environment, the characters. They may place themselves in the storyteller's position, imagining and possibly thinking about their own responses to the events. In this situation both participants are active; they may visibly interact as the listener nods or provides a verbal response such as a question. For these reasons the process of storytelling in itself is a social one.

Psychological studies have also been conducted that support the notion that there is a close relationship between story and social activity; these studies found that story-telling and their understanding connected to part of the brain associated with social processing (Saxe and Wexler, 2005; Lieberman, 2007).

The social aspect of storytelling appears to fulfil numerous functions. A particular aspect of social behaviour that has been strongly connected to story is that of culture (Bruner, 1990; Moon, 2010).

Schein defines culture as

A pattern of shared basic assumptions, invented, discovered or developed by any given group as it learns to cope with its problems of external adaptation and internal integration that has worked well enough to be considered valid and therefore is taught to new members of the group as the correct way to think and feel in relation to those problems – reframing.

(Schein, 1987, p 31)

Schein's definition illustrates that any group possesses culture. The definition also shows that culture has an influence on behaviour; it presents group members with expectations on how to behave, particularly in relation to difficulties they may face.

Culture is often disseminated in explicit rules, for example legislation. It is also passed on through traditional practice. As articulated previously in this chapter, social constructivists believe that learning is built over time and is influenced by individual experience. However, social constructivists also recognise that this experi-ence occurs in a social world, and therefore a person's experience is affected by those around them (Dewey, 1938). Writers such as Lave and Wenger (1991) have emphasised the social nature of learning. As culture is so influential on group/social behaviour it can also affect learning. In recognition of the impact social environments have on learning, Lave and Wenger stress the importance of context. New arrivals to a particular context learn from more established group members through their inter-action with them. Sternberg et al (2000) express similar ideas to Lave and Wenger regarding the social nature of learning and the influence of context. Sternberg and colleagues talk of practical intelligence; this is the tacit knowledge that accrues within the workplace and importantly they stress that it is immersion in everyday life that is necessary for the acquisition of this knowledge.

Lave and Wenger provide some insights into how established group members indicate to novices the expectations of behaviour (prevailing culture) within a certain setting.

Particular tools are used and are important for this purpose. For example, workplace policies provide detail of relevant rules and are commonly discussed during the induction of new recruits or students. Work routines, often evolving through traditional practice, indicate to staff the requirements of them in both time and space. 'Artefacts' are also considered to be of significance. The term 'artefacts' includes objects such as workplace diaries; these objects may be viewed with some reverence as they are so key in determining the requirements from different staff members during a particular day. Nevertheless, it is social interaction and active participation that is key to learning, establishing group membership and development of expertise (Lave and Wenger, 1991); therefore, it is reasonable to suggest that story will be essential in this process.

Bruner (1990) supports the connection between transmission of culture and storytelling. Bruner uses the term *'folk psychology'* (p 35) to explain the connection. Folk psychology is *'a set of more or less connected, more or less normative descriptions about how human beings tick'* (p 35). Folk psychology is often called common sense and it is learned through story. Both Bruner (1990) and Moon (2010) describe how each person has a repository of stories, some may be acquired through direct experience others through story sharing; however, each one has potential to offer assistance in the interpretation of novel situations. Bruner (1990) illustrates how this process works from a US perspective using the following example. A person enters a store waving the union flag. In order to understand this situation, an observer will utilise their repertoire of stories for a possible explanation. Possibilities include: it is a public holiday; there is a fundraiser; it is an eccentric person. The story most closely resembling the new experience will influence the choice of response to it.

The social nature of learning, the influence of culture on group behaviour and the contribution that storytelling makes to the transmission of culture demonstrates the importance of story in the field. Stories can assist the learner in understanding the expectations of the setting; they can facilitate active participation because they involve interaction, and according to Lave and Wenger it is this active participation that is fundamental to learning. Importantly, stories can provide novices with ideas on appropriate responses to possible dilemmas. This is achieved by more experienced colleagues demonstrating appropriate responses through their storytelling.

Schein's definition also recognises how human beings can exist within different cultures. Indeed, most of us do operate within different groups. For example, we live within families whose members have certain expectations of us. Students attend their educational institution and have involvement in groups within the field such as a social work team. It is possible that different cultures will impact on each other. Wenger alludes to this in his work on Communities of Practice (1999). He acknowledges that when different Communities of Practice have contact there will be some knowledge exchange; this could include material that incorporates expectations of behaviour/cultural information. Under these circumstances the culture of one setting may impact on the culture of another. Students exchanging stories of practice in the field within the higher education setting indicated that there may be some filtering of information (Flanagan, 2015). This may have been influenced by cultural expectations of the educational institution regarding acceptable behaviour but may also be due to the influence of a wider professional culture. In this sense, story sharing within small groups can assist in the dissemination and reinforcement of broader cultural expectations such as those possessed by a profession.

Providing individuals with insights into the expectations of group behaviour can facilitate group cohesion. Group cohesion is also thought to be facilitated by story through the act of sharing, for example, sharing ideas and experiences (Moon, 2010). Story has been found to encourage active participation; it was also associated with students sharing something of themselves (Flanagan, 2015). As stories are so fundamental to an individual's interpretation of their world (Ricoeur, 1984), the sharing of a story inevitably reveals something about the storyteller. Also, observations of storytelling within higher education (Flanagan, 2015) revealed that participants shared stories relating to their personal life as well as their work life, such as events from childhood, experiences of parenting. These revelations may help participants get to know each other. Participants also linked the stories heard during class with humour and on observation the stories shared were commonly associated with laughter. Not surprisingly, students linked storytelling with an opportunity to relax.

Task 4.4 Task for students

Think about an induction process that you have experienced. Did it make reference to some of the tools Lave and Wenger mention? For example, were you informed of a certain policy that was considered key? Were there certain artefacts that were of significance?

Reflect on your interaction with experienced colleagues. Do you recall team members sharing stories of their experiences? These stories may have contained appropriate solutions to possible dilemmas; they may also have transmitted to you indications of responses that are considered appropriate forms of conduct for staff members within that particular setting.

Was there a particular story that will stay with you, one that you think is transferable for future practice experience? It may be useful to jot some examples down in your reflective journal and contemplate why a particular story resonates so much for you. Also reflect on the stories shared between fellow learners; how do you feel they impact on your learning.

Stories appear to contribute significantly to group cohesion not only through their ability to reveal the prevailing group culture but through their association with sharing, humour and relaxation. These characteristics of story are particularly valuable in practice where effective team working is so important.

Again, when reflecting on your placement experiences think about when story may have been used for these purposes. For example, did somebody provide a particularly funny story that helped to reduce possible tensions within the team?

The ingredients of engaging story and storytelling

Having recognised the valuable contribution that story can make to learning, reflection and the social impact of story, it would be useful to determine the characteristics of an engaging story and an effective storyteller.

There is some agreement that reoccurring themes are present within stories. Stories contain characters and plots (Bruner, 1987; Ricoeur, 1990). Taylor et al (2002) describe how a good story includes a chronology of events that contain both the unusual and the mundane. Propp (1968) performed a structural analysis of mainly European fairy tales. He concluded that fairy stories handed down over many years possessed repetitive ready-made formulae. Propp claimed that although contemporary stories appear more complex and varied in their structure, if they were studied over the passage of time there would be a similar result. Taylor et al (2002) believed that there were certain characteristics that made a story particularly appealing: characters are important, the language and the setting is also considered significant and stories should offer insights into human activity. Students stated that the main reason a story held interest for them was if they could connect to it and it held meaning, if it felt familiar and they could see themselves in that situation. For example, the solution to a potential problem. Valuable stories also evoked emotion, usually humour (Flanagan, 2015).

The storyteller was seen as significant in their ability to influence the quality of a story (Flanagan, 2015). This was mostly associated with the storyteller's capacity to deliver the characteristics of a good story, including meaning and emotion. Significantly, interesting stories needed some credibility. This appears inconsistent with the recognition from students that not all stories shared within higher education are completely factual. A possible explanation for this is that accounts of experience shared by students within higher education are recognised as stories through their narrative structure; they may even be introduced as a story. This could encourage students to respond to them in a certain way, as Moon stated, to *'suspend their disbelief'* (2010, p 63). This results in students being satisfied in the credibility of a story if it felt plausible rather than if it was true.

Despite the ability of stories to create learning and evoke a response in a recipient, there is recognition that judgements on the quality of a story will vary and not all stories will captivate all recipients. The individual nature of our cognitive structures can explain the rejection of some stories because they do not connect with the listener. The influence of the storyteller is significant, particularly for students in a group learning situation where some group members may not feel comfortable in story sharing, they may lack confidence and this can impact on their ability to deliver their message.

Ideas on the characteristics of an engaging story and the skills of the storyteller do have implications for the placement experience. They help explain why placements can resonate for students as they make connections between the interpretations of their new experience and their previous understanding.

Acceptance of the fundamental links between story and experiential understanding and acknowledgement that stories can create different responses in the individual helps to explain why student experiences can vary, for example, two students may be with the same team but have differing views on the quality of their placement experience. Stories help explain why some placement events can resonate strongly for students as they make connections between the interpretations of their new experience and their previous understanding.

The ingredients of engaging stories reveal how placements can create emotions in students when they interact with those around them and how important tacit information, which helps facilitate group cohesion and a sense of belonging in the student, may be conveyed to them via the overall meaning of a shared story.

To conclude, as Moon claims, story surrounds our everyday experiences. It is a crucial resource for our understanding of them and our subsequent learning. Stories appeal to our unique nature but also facilitate sharing and connections to those significant others who contribute to our day-to-day lives. In recognition of these positive qualities, it is valuable to pause at times and remember the contributions of this phenomenon which can occur so often and so naturally for many of us that we forget its presence.

References

Alterio, M (2004) Collaborative Journalling as a Professional Development Tool. *Journal of Further and Higher Education*, 28 (3): 321–32.

Atkins, A and Murphy, K (1993) Reflection: A Review of the Literature. *Journal of Advanced Nursing*, 18: 1188–92.

Bolton, G (2006) *Reflective Practice: Writing and Professional Development* (2nd ed). London: Sage.

Bruner, J (1986) *Actual Minds, Possible Worlds.* London: Harvard University Press.

Bruner, J (1987) Life as Narrative. *Social Research*, 54(1): 11–32.

Bruner, J (1990) *Acts of Meaning.* London: Harvard University Press.

Carr, D (1991) Discussion: Ricoeur on Narrative, in Wood, D (ed) *On Paul Ricoeur: Narrative and Interpretation.* London, Routledge.

Chan, E A and Chung, L Y F (2004) Teaching Abstract Concepts in Contemporary Nursing Through Spirituality. *Reflective Practice*, 5(1): 125–32.

Dewey, J (1938) The Influence of Darwin on Philosophy and Other Essays on Contemporary Thought, in McDermott, J (ed) (1981) *The Philosophy of John Dewey Two Volumes in One. 1 The Structure of Experience; 2 Lived Experience.* Chicago: University of Chicago Press.

Douglas, K and Carless, D (2009) Exploring Taboo Issues in Professional Sport Through a Fictional Approach. *Reflective Practice*, 10(3): 311–23.

Flanagan, S (2015) How Does Storytelling Within Higher Education Contribute to the Learning Experience of Early Years Students? *Journal of Practice Teaching and Learning*, 13(2–3): 146–68.

Flecknoe, M (2001) *Writing a Reflective Journal.* Leeds Metropolitan University [video: VHS].

Frid, I, Ohlen, J and Bergbom, I (2000) On the Use of Narratives in Nursing Research. *Journal of Advanced Nursing*, 32(3): 695–703.

Gabriel, Y (2000) *Storytelling in Organisations.* Oxford: Oxford University Press.

Gibbs, G (1988) *Learning by Doing: A Guide to Teaching and Learning Methods.* London: FEU.

Gold, J and Holman, D (2001) Let Me Tell You a Story: An Evaluation of the Use of Storytelling and Argument Analysis in Management Education. *Career Development International*, 6(7): 384–95.

Goleman, D (1996) Emotional Intelligence: Why It Can Matter More than IQ. *Learning*, 24(6): 49–50.

Harrison, K (2009) Listen: This Really Happened: Making Sense of Social Work Through Story-Telling. *Social Work Education*, 28(7): 750–64.

Hoggan, C and Cranton, P (2015) Promoting Transformative Learning Through Reading Fiction. *Journal of Transformative Education*, 13(1): 6–25.

Husserl, E (1964) *The Phenomenology of Internal Time Consciousness.* Trans Churchill, J S with an introduction by Schrag, C O. Bloomington, IN, Indiana University Press.

Kolb, D (1984) *Experiential Learning: Experience as the Source of Learning and Development.* Englewood Cliffs, NJ: Prentice Hall.

Lave, J and Wenger, E (1991) *Situated Learning: Legitimate Peripheral Participation.* Cambridge: Cambridge University Press.

Lieberman, M (2007) Social Cognitive Neuroscience: A Review of Core Processes. *Annual Review of Psychology*, 22: 415–50.

McDrury, J and Alterio, M (2002) *Learning Through Storytelling: Using Reflection and Experience in Higher Education Contexts.* Palmerston North, New Zealand: The Dunmore Press Limited.

McEwan, H and Egan, K (1995) *Narrative in Teaching, Learning and Research.* New York: Teachers College, Columbia University.

Moon, J (2010) *Using Story in Higher Education and Professional Development.* London: Routledge.

Moon, J and Fowler, J (2008) There Is a Story to Be Told: A Framework for the Conception of Story in Higher Education and Professional Development. *Nurse Education Today*, 28 (2): 232–39.

Noddings, N (1996) Stories and Affect in Teacher Education. *Cambridge Journal of Education*, 26(3): 435–48.

Piaget, J (1971) *Biology and Knowledge.* Edinburgh: Edinburgh University Press. Cited in Moon, J (2010) *Using Story in Higher Education and Professional Development.* London, Routledge.

Propp, V (1968) *Morphology of the Folktale.* Austin, Texas: University of Texas Press.

Ricoeur, P (1984) *Time and Narrative* (vol 1). Chicago: University of Chicago Press.

Ricoeur, P (1990) *Time and Narrative* (vol 3). Chicago: University of Chicago Press.

Saxe, R and Wexler, A (2005) Making Sense of Another Mind: The Role of the Right Tempero-Parietal Junction. *Neuropsychologia*, 43: 1391–99.

Schein, E H (1987) Defining Organizational Culture, in Shafritz, J and Ott, S (eds) *Classics of Organizational Theory* (2nd ed) (pp 381–96). Chicago: The Dorsey Press. Cited in Bellot, J (2011) Defining and Assessing Organizational Culture. Nursing Forum, 46(1): 29–37.

Schön, D (1983) *The Reflective Practitioner.* San Francisco: Jossey Bass.

Sternberg, R, Forsythe, G, Hedlund, J, Horvath, J, Wanger, R, Williams, W, Snook, S and Grorenko, E (2000) *Practical Intelligence in Everyday Life.* Cambridge: Cambridge University Press.

Taylor, C (2006) Narrating Significant Experience: Reflective Accounts and the Production of (Self) Knowledge. *British Journal of Social Work*, 36: 189–206.

Taylor, S, Fisher, D and Dufresne, R (2002) The Aesthetics of Management Storytelling. *Management Learning*, 33(3): 313–30.

Trought, F (2012) *Brilliant Employability Skills: How to Stand Out from the Crowd in the Graduate Job Market.* Harlow: Prentice Hall.

Webster, L and Mertova, P (2007) *Using Narrative Inquiry as a Research Method: An Introduction to Using Critical Event Narrative Analysis in Research on Learning and Teaching.* London: Routledge.

Wenger, E (1999) *Communities of Practice: Learning Meaning and Identity.* Cambridge: Cambridge University Press.

Chapter 5

Applying law in practice: Weapon, tool, manual or barrier?

Allan Norman

The first thing we do, let's kill all the lawyers.

Henry VI Part II, Act 4, scene 2, William Shakespeare

'Everything is lawful,' but not everything is beneficial. 'Everything is lawful,' but not everything builds others up.

1 Corinthians 10:23, Christian Bible

Introduction: 'Everything is lawful' – maybe ...

There is a question I sometimes pose, in order to invite reflection upon attitudes to authority generally, and to legal authority in particular. Do you believe that by default you are entitled to do anything unless it is expressly forbidden, or that you are forbidden from doing anything unless it is expressly permitted? Your answer will reflect to what extent you see yourself as the holder of rights, or as a person subject to obligations.

A supplementary question might potentially invite a different answer: do you believe that a local authority, or a social worker working for a local authority, is entitled to do anything unless it is expressly forbidden, or is forbidden from doing anything unless it is expressly permitted?

I say that the supplementary question might potentially invite a different answer, because historically it could be said that as individuals we were generally free to do anything that was not forbidden, but that local authorities were limited to the powers expressly granted to them by law, and therefore needed to be clear of the authority for anything they did.

It is no longer the case that local authorities, and the social workers working for them, can do nothing except that which is expressly permitted. The Local Government Act 2000 introduced a 'well-being power', which expressly permitted local authorities to do anything to promote well-being that was not otherwise forbidden. For a social work practitioner, or a student on placement, that reversed the previous presumption: no

Table 5.1 Philosophy and plumbing compared

	Philosophy	Plumbing
Content of materials	Evaluative	Descriptive
Law is reviewed	Critically	Uncritically
Law is a tool for	Change	Certainty
Students should be competent	Thinkers	Technicians
Attitude to user challenges	Assistance	Avoidance

longer was it necessary to ask, 'where is the permission to do this?'; it became sufficient to ask 'is there anything stopping me doing this?' The Localism Act 2011 extended and replaced the well-being principle with a more general principle that local authorities have the power to do anything that individuals can do.

These presumptions of lawfulness carry little reassurance for many students or practitioners. For many, the law is overwhelming and ubiquitous in its scope, and its practice and its conclusions are difficult to understand, so little comfort can be gained from an assertion that there is a presumption of lawfulness: there are simply too many unknown pitfalls to avoid. Given this ubiquity, the social work student on placement is going to encounter the law, and their attitude to the law may well be shaped by what they observe on placement.

Braye and Preston-Shoot (2005, p 15) reflected on the question of why social workers needed to study law, and used the analogy of 'Pericles and the plumber' (Twining, 1967) to compare and contrast two possible answers. The plumbing analogy reflects the idea of legal competence requiring knowledge of the law and the ability to use it to achieve social work's ends, while Pericles embodied the value of critical thinking and reflection on how the law intrudes into social work practice. This dichotomy may be characterised as shown in Table 5.1.

Here, I have branched out to consider four ways of conceptualising the relationship, and with a particular focus upon the student placement experience. Specifically, I explore how the student may encounter the law being used or conceived as a weapon, a tool, a manual, or a barrier in social work practice. I suggest a model for student and practitioner to reflect upon how the law is used; and provide my own reflections upon what a healthy relationship with the law might look like.

It's not all about law: Let's not kill all the lawyers

An understanding of law is compulsory for the social work student. The requirement has arisen out of historic concerns arising out of research (Ball et al, 1988) and service failures, that social workers have failed to demonstrate an adequate understanding. When the Diploma in Social Work was introduced, legal knowledge was the one area where there was specific and detailed guidance about what should be covered and how it should be assessed (CCETSW, 1995). Recent social work standards documents explicitly refer to the requirement to have an understanding of the law.

In particular, the Standards of Proficiency for Social Workers in England (HCPC, 2017) require at Standard 2 that social workers are *'able to practise within the legal and ethical boundaries of their profession'*, which includes the following:

2.1 *understand current legislation applicable to social work with adults, children, young people and families*

2.5 *be able to manage and weigh up competing or conflicting values or interests to make reasoned professional judgements*

2.6 *be able to exercise authority as a social worker within the appropriate legal and ethical frameworks and boundaries*

2.7 *understand the need to respect and so far as possible uphold, the rights, dignity, values and autonomy of every service user and carer*

2.8 *recognise that relationships with service users and carers should be based on respect and honesty*

2.9 *recognise the power dynamics in relationships with service users and carers, and be able to manage those dynamics appropriately*

My selection of these parts of that standard is intended to reflect that the requirement to understand law is interwoven with an understanding of the nature of professional judgement, of power and authority, of ethics, and of rights, among other things. The priority given to the different parts of this Proficiency Standard may well affect whether law becomes weaponised, seen neutrally as a tool or manual, or perceived negatively as a barrier.

The reference in the opening of this chapter to *'authority generally, and to legal authority in particular'* reflects that when I introduce students to law, I start not with the idea of the law, but the concept of legal authority. This can convey both that it is a characteristic of law that it carries some kind of authority, and also that the law is not alone in possessing that characteristic. In turn, to view law as carrying some kind of authority invites thinking about the nature of law, and indeed critical thinking about whether and why the law should carry authority.

Rodriguez-Blanco (2014, p 11) observes:

Law transforms our lives in the most important way: it changes how we act and because of this it gives rise to fundamental questions. One such question concerns legal authority and individual autonomy and asks: if we are autonomous agents how do legislators, judges and officials have legitimate authority to change our actions and indirectly change how we conduct our lives?

This question, posed in respect of the relationship between law and the individual, takes on an added piquancy when revisited in the context of the relationship between law and social work: is social work an autonomous profession if its actions are tightly bound within the four corners of a restrictive legal framework? Ife (2012, p 12) observes that the social work role manifests itself in different ways throughout the world, but that:

In societies such as that of the United Kingdom, social work has been seen as the implementation of the policies of the welfare state through the provision of statutory services ...

Social work in the United Kingdom is thereby singled out as an example of a model constrained within the legislative framework and purpose. Social workers and students will need to be particularly astute to understand the framework of legal authority which governs their role.

One approach to opening up the different kinds of authority which the social work student will encounter is to consider the different types of question that might invite reflection in a practice situation. Table 5.2 introduces, alongside legal authority, some of the other kinds of questions that the law is not appropriately placed to address.

Table 5.2 Different sources of authority

Law	What am I allowed or required to do?
Ethics	What is the right thing to do?
Research/Evidence-Based Practice	What has been observed to happen? What works?
Professional Standards and Codes	What is considered professional behaviour?
Comparative Practice	How is it done elsewhere?
Government Policy	What does the government want me to do?
Policies and Procedures	What do other people want me to do?

Students arriving on placement may have been taught law in a variety of different ways. In some institutions, legal knowledge and understanding is integrated throughout the course; in others, it is a discrete element of the course (Braye and Preston-Shoot, 2005, pp 23–4). In some institutions, law is taught alongside ethics (Braye and Preston-Shoot, 2005, p 66). In others – and indeed within the pages of this book – law and policy are grouped together. Sometimes, law is compartmentalised, with the law relating to different areas of social work practice separated out.

Table 5.2 invites certain reflections on the law with which the student arrives equipped on placement. If law and ethics for example are answering different kinds of question, then they might not point towards the same conclusion as to the right way for the social work student or practitioner to act. Practitioners cannot always avoid such dilemmas. Take, for example, the Withholding and Withdrawal of Support Regulations 2002. As their name hints, these regulations require social workers to withhold or withdraw social services support from certain categories of individuals on the basis of their immigration status. This is legislation, but there is good reason to think that there might be some conflict between such a legal obligation and one's ethical or professional obligations. Humphries (2004) powerfully articulates that social workers operating such laws:

... have not resisted the gate-keeping and inhumane role thrust upon them. It is no wonder they are despised and feared by the people they purport to help. We can safely regard the rhetoric about anti-oppressive and anti-racist practice as harmless delusion.

If, however, law is no more than a manual telling you how to perform the social work role, then there might be no critical engagement between legal and other forms of authority such as professional and ethical authority.

A similar point might be made in relation to research into the effectiveness of different forms of intervention: the fact that a particular form of intervention is shown to be effective does not necessarily mean that it is ethical, nor that it is lawful.

Law and policy are so frequently elided that it might be surprising within Table 5.2 to see the suggestion that they are answering very different kinds of questions, and indeed that policies seem to be held out as having little authority. That, however, is an important point for the student to grasp. Policies and procedures play a prominent role within many agencies in shaping practice. Sometimes they are indeed conflated with the law in the practitioner's imagination. However, the critical and reflective practitioner will understand that policies do not in themselves have any legal authority, and will reflect on issues of ethics, professional role, rights etc rather than turning uncritically to an agency policy as a manual determining how to act.

> ## Task 5.1 Task for students
>
> Using your reflective journal, consider an agency policy document to which you have been directed by your practice educator.
>
> » Do you know whether the document has any legal authority to tell you what you can or must do?
>
> » If it does, can you identify from where it derives its legal authority?
>
> » If it does not, do you know whether it is correctly reflects the law? How do you know?
>
> » Do you consider that you are obliged to follow what the policy document says? Your answer to this question might include reflections upon the authority of the policy, whether it is permissive or mandatory in nature; whether there are other legal considerations that you consider would carry greater authority in deciding how to act; and whether you consider other considerations such as professional and ethical practice might conflict with the policy.
>
> ### Task for practice educators
>
> Be prepared to discuss the reflections arising from the policy document considered.

Answering the 'but is it the law?' question

Thus far, legal authority has been distinguished from other forms of authority, and it has been posited that reflective practice which identifies these distinctions will help to show where there may be conflicts to be addressed. However, conflicts are not confined to inconsistencies between legal and other forms of authority. Sometimes different forms of legal authority seem to be inconsistent with each other. In order to better understand this, it may be helpful to consider the various forms of legal authority the practitioner or student is likely to encounter.

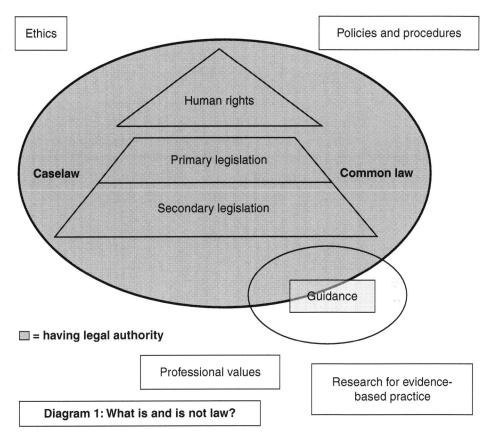

= having legal authority

Diagram 1: What is and is not law?

When considering the PCF (I have chosen the 'End of First Placement' level, which reflects the level students should have achieved in between their two primary placements), the relevant parts around legal understanding are generally located within the domain 'Rights and Justice'. This includes the following:

*Social workers recognise the fundamental principles of **human rights** and equality, and that these are protected in national and international law, conventions and policies. They ensure these principles underpin their practice. Social workers understand the importance of using and contributing to **case law** and applying these rights in their own practice. They understand the effects of oppression, discrimination and poverty.*

» *Understand and, with support, apply in practice the principles of social justice, inclusion and equality.*

» *Understand how **legislation** and **guidance** can advance or constrain people's rights.*

» *Work within the principles of human and civil rights and equalities legislation.* [my emphasis]

Within this framework, we can see reference to each of (a) human rights including those protected in international law; (b) legislation; (c) guidance; and (d) caselaw. It will be observed that each of these is also reflected within the grey shaded area of the diagram, as distinct sources of law.

Pausing to further reflect, those parts represented diagrammatically within the triangle and trapezium of diagram 1 are intended to reflect a certain hierarchy of legal authority. Human rights tops this hierarchy. A lawyer might say this is because the Human Rights Act 1998 is a piece of constitutional legislation, super-charged as it provides a lens through which all other legislation previously and subsequently must be viewed and interpreted. A social worker might also want human rights to top the hierarchy, but for different reasons.

The international definition of social work (IFSW, 2014) includes the affirmation that *'human rights … are central to social work'*. The PCF describes those principles as *'fundamental'*, as the international definition also did prior to 2014 (IFSW, 2000), and places legal understanding within an explicit framework of rights and justice. Social work has frequently been explicitly framed as a human rights profession (United Nations, 1994; Ife, 2001; Healy, 2008) and one might hope that a rights-based approach would prevail in practice.

Neither caselaw nor common law have been placed in a hierarchical relationship with other forms of legal authority in diagram 1. Both are essentially judge-made law. The latter is used in particular in relation to judicial decision-making in areas where there is not a clear legislative framework, or there is a lacuna in it. Caselaw embraces a wide range of circumstances, including where the judge has to decide the meaning of contested statutory provisions.

As indicated, the social work student is expected by the PCF to use and, curiously, contribute to caselaw. These categories of judge-made law can be problematic for the student, because caselaw ignores the many circumstances in which the law is uncontested, and because of how it focuses upon disputes rather than uncontentious practice. It also ignores reasons why the law may be uncontested, for example the difficulties that service users might have in actually accessing justice and the courts. It can present a jaundiced view of social work practice. Caselaw is unlikely to set out critically what is wrong with the law itself, although social work students should be alive to that. There can be randomness and unpredictability around which cases come before a court, and in particular courts can be ill-suited to deal with collective interests.

On the other hand, caselaw is the mechanism to resolve ambiguities in the law. It flags up where the problems have arisen in real life, which can be real danger areas for practitioners (the misuse of section 20 of the Children Act in relation to children and families practice, or of the Deprivation of Liberty Safeguards in relation to practice with adults being examples). It also sets out a coherent framework for considering all the other kinds of legal authority and trying to reconcile them, providing models of legal thinking that might be useful to the practitioner. Learning through caselaw can be less dry than through study of legislation policy and guidance, because it amounts to learning from real life. Finally, common law in particular is alive to finding solutions to social work problems that legislation has not adequately addressed (radicalisation and grooming injunctions being examples in relation to children and families practice; safeguarding adults from coercion and undue influence is an example in relation to practice with adults).

Returning to the diagrammatic representation of legal authority on page 65, guidance straddles the boundary between what is and is not law. This reflects in particular the curious status of statutory guidance, a form of guidance whose early development was located within social work practice, under section 7 of the Local Authority Social Services Act 1970 – although many more pieces of legislation now authorise the creation of statutory guidance. Statutory guidance is a curious hybrid: if it gained its authority from legislation, then in what sense is it merely guidance; but on the other hand if it is in fact guidance, then how can it be said to have legal authority? This dilemma was addressed (in something of a fudge) in R v Islington LBC ex parte Rixon (1998) 1 CCLR 119:

Parliament by section 7(1) has required local authorities to follow the path charted by the secretary of state's guidance, with liberty to deviate from it where the local authority judges on admissible grounds that there is good reason to do so, but without freedom to take a substantially different course.

I suggested that there may be conflicts between different forms of legal authority, as well as with other forms of authority. A practice dilemma that illustrates this concerns whether a practitioner in the field of adult community care might invoke safeguarding procedures to protect an adult from self-neglect. There is a legal framework to do so in respect of an adult who lacks the mental capacity to make the relevant decisions. More generally, the Care Act 2014 provides a framework that requires intervention where there is a risk of neglect, but without defining it. The statutory guidance defines it with reference to self-neglect among other forms of neglect, but the suggestion that this might give rise to a duty to protect an adult who has the capacity to make a decision, and the right to make an unwise decision, might seem to run counter to the principles of mental capacity legislation, while more broadly the suggestion that the social worker can intervene in the best interests of a person who does not wish it, would be constrained by human rights principles. The practitioner encountering such a scenario is therefore going to need to address not only the conflict between legal authority and other principles such as professional values and research, but also the unresolved tensions within the law itself.

> ## Task 5.2 Task for students
>
> Using your reflective journal, consider creatively and imaginatively a form of intervention that might be beneficial to a service user with whom you are working. Reflect on whether you can actually uses that intervention with the service user or not. Consider separately what issues would arise if the service user would welcome your intervention, and if they would not.
>
> If the service user would welcome the intervention, then the well-being power discussed suggests that you have the legal authority to do it, unless it is expressly prohibited. Are you able to identify anything in the law that prohibits it? Are you able to identify anything outside of the law, such as local authority practice, resource constraints, or ethical issues that might tend to count against it?
>
> If the service user would not welcome the intervention, can you identify the legal authority that might allow you to pursue this intervention nonetheless? Even where you can, does the law in question permit you or does it require you to do so? Do any other legal considerations, such as human rights considerations, tend to point towards a different conclusion?
>
> Throughout, try to ensure you consider all the different types of legal authority – rights, legislation, judge-made law and statutory guidance – that might impact upon your decision.
>
> ### Task for practice educators
>
> Be prepared to discuss the reflections arising from the intervention being proposed. If the intervention would be welcomed by the service user and is not legally contra-indicated, would you be prepared to try to facilitate actually delivering it? If the intervention would be unwelcome, and is not legally contra-indicated, would you still be prepared to consider it? Be ready to feedback on these in a subsequent session.

Weapons and barriers: Extreme ends of the spectrum or mirror images?

Having arrived at a point where it can be understood that there are a few clearly delineated sources of law that the social worker needs to be aware of, but that there may well be conflict within them, or between them and other sources of authority that we believe ought to affect our social work decision-making, it might pay to revisit the earlier observation that social workers do not feel confident around the law. It might not be simply that law is another discipline; it might be that the nature of law's authority creates conflicts that we would rather not have to resolve.

I suspect the idea of weaponising the law is one that we can readily understand. If someone quotes law at us, or even a legal phrase, we tend to assume that there must be some legal authority for what the person is saying, which they probably understand better than us; or at least that we are unlikely to get anywhere arguing a contrary position. The legal authority might be contested. 'Data protection' and 'health and safety', for example, are frequently cited by people who could not distinguish the law from the policies that have been devised to give effect to it. The Health and Safety Executive even has a mythbuster website (www.hse.gov.uk/myth/), compiling its responses to the many astonishing claims made for health and safety law. If the policy goes further than the law, however, arguing against the policy may still be an unfruitful venture.

Bilson (2018) highlights how some Local Safeguarding Children Boards have policies which require a section 47 enquiry when bruising is found in pre-mobile babies. That is not a requirement of the Children Act, nor of the relevant statutory guidance. Moreover, it would appear to constrain the application of professional judgement. Bilson, reviewing both the research and the policies, observes that *'research evidence is limited and contradictory, but even the lowest findings of accidental bruising suggest that it is likely to happen many times more frequently than maltreatment'* (p 7). I am not seeking here to deconstruct either the policies or the research, simply to observe that the policies automatically drive a legal intervention – the section 47 enquiry – but the parents who encounter that enquiry will experience it as a legal process, rather than the local application of a policy. I suggest we are weaponising the law when we use the language and processes of the law to justify interventions that we might not be legally required to pursue.

The more legally literate service users, or those who are somehow able to gain access to legal advice, may in turn weaponise the law against a social worker. An articulate complaint, especially one plausibly framed in legal language, might be effective to stop a course of action in its tracks, sometimes even to bring about a change of social worker. I suggest that the following characteristically suggest that the law is being used as a weapon:

> » Where legal language is used to secure compliance with a course of action, irrespective of whether the law necessarily indicates that the course of action must be followed.

» Where legal language is used to suggest that a course of action is manda-tory, when in fact relevant law is permissive in nature, allows for discretion, or requires the exercise of professional judgement.

» Where legal language is used to deny access to services, when in fact the relevant law is permissive in nature, allows for discretion, or requires the exercise of professional judgement.

This kind of weaponising is likely to be contract-indicated by Professional Standards 2.8 and 2.9 above.

However, if the service user is also able to use the law in this way, it might be argued that the perception of the law as a weapon or a barrier simply reflects mirror images each of the other, so that when the law is a weapon in the hands of the social worker it is a barrier to the service user, and vice versa. An additional dimension to add in here concerns whether services are wanted by the service user or not. For example, parents of children in need including children with disabilities, and adults with care and support needs or their carers, might be actively seeking services from a social worker, and the weaponising of the law might be in the use of the law and its processes to *deny* the services that they seek.

This might be expressed as shown in Table 5.3.

Table 5.3 Attitudes to the law, filtered by whether services are wanted, and whose perspective is considered

		Perspective of	
		Service user	**Social worker**
Services are ...	**Wanted**	Law is positive if it gives rise to eligibility or rights to services; it is problematic if there is unchallengeable professional discretion or ineligibility.	Law is positive if I can provide the help that I feel is appropriate within my professional judgement; it is problematic if I am required to withhold help or to provide it where other considerations such as resources or the rights of others contra-indicate the help.
	Unwanted	Law is positive if my rights encompass the right to reject the intervention or challenge its implementation; it is problematic if I can be compelled to accept the unwanted intervention.	Law is positive if the service user can be compelled to accept the intervention and my professional judgement is that they should; it is problematic if their rights leave me unable to do what in my professional judgement is right.

Table 5.4 Law as a weapon and barrier contrasted

	Weapon	↔	Barrier
Engagement with transparency	Low	↔	High
Relationship to service user	Controlling	↔	Fearful
Law is presented to students ...	Uncritically	↔	Critically
Legal ambiguity is seen as ...	Problematic	↔	Helpful
Likely relationship to legal proceedings	Initiating	↔	Defending
Social work seen as relatively ...	Powerful	↔	Powerless
Perceived effect of the law on available alternatives	Extends	↔	Constrains
Challenge by service users is ...	Avoided	↔	Accepted

Within the fourfold conceptualisation of law as potentially constituting a weapon, tool, manual or barrier, I have constructed the weapon and barrier as being extremes, while noting that how the law is characterised might depend upon whose perspective is being considered, and whether services are wanted or unwanted.

In particular, I suggested that there can be unethical elements of a lack of transparency about the limits of power and authority when law is used as a weapon, and a failure of lateral thinking when it is seen as a barrier. Good social work practice invites being open about service users' rights as well as about social workers' obligations, about the limits to social work's authority, and about access to remedies that would enable practice to be tested. Social work practice gains its proper legitimacy when it is able to achieve its results notwithstanding being transparent about the limits upon social workers' power and authority. This is quite apparent from Standard 2.8 on respect and honesty, and Standard 2.9 on power dynamics. Equally, the PCF which frames legal understanding within the framework of anti-oppressive and anti-discriminatory practice, built on rights and equality, and recognising that the law can both advance and constrain good practice, reflects the same concerns. Conceptualisation of the law as either a tool or a manual enables such concerns to be addressed.

Task 5.3 Task for students and practice educators

Proficiency Standard 9.3 requires social workers to assist service users *'to understand and exercise their rights'*. Reflect what this might mean in practice.

Service users' rights include their legal rights, and their legal rights include their legal rights to question, test or challenge your decisions to provide or to withhold services. Are you confident that you sufficiently understand their rights to challenge you? Given that a service user's rights include their right to access a range of remedies and not only a complaints procedure, are you confident to advise on the range of remedies that they might use? Given that you may be unable to advise independently on such remedies, how could you help your service user to obtain independent advice and assistance to pursue their remedies in respect of the decisions that you have made about them?

Tools and manuals: What is the difference?

To conceive of the law as a tool or as a manual may be perceived as a less questioning approach to the law. After all, if these conceptions equates to Twining's (1967) 'plumbing' approach, the emphasis is upon a functional understanding of how the law can support social work's objects, rather than upon problematising the law. However, as Braye and Preston-Shoot (2005, p 17) observe, being able to use the law competently, and being able to evaluate the law critically, are not mutually exclusive alternatives.

The primary difference between tools and manuals, or my purpose in proposing that there is such a difference, relates to the difference between social work's ends, and the means by which it pursues those ends. A lawyer may equate these to substantive law (which emphasises the end result that the law seeks to achieve, or the mischief it seeks to address) and procedural law (which emphasises the process must be followed in order to achieve that end).

Accordingly, social workers perceiving the law as a tool are interested in how it can assist in achieving social work's ends, while the conception of the law as a manual sees it as prescribing the steps that must be taken. Understanding the relationship between these two is important. In many areas, lawyers might argue that the right outcome is that which results from the application of the fair process. Thus, for example, unless a person can be convicted through a fair trial, it is right that they are not convicted: a belief in guilt should not lead to a twisting of, or interference with, the process so as to achieve a conviction at all costs. Closer to home, judicial review is a legal process that is often applied to scrutinise social work decision-making, a process that has been described as *'the judge over your shoulder'* (TSol, 2006). Judicial review applies principles of administrative law that set out what fair decision-making looks like. The remedy presupposes that you cannot be confident that an outcome was fair in circumstances where the process leading to that outcome was not fair. Those principles apply to decision-making by social workers, so that some social work training programmes explicitly embody them within law teaching (Braye and Preston-Shoot, 2005, p 66).

It is instructive for the social work student to reflect upon both what those principles do say, and what they do not say, about how social work achieves its ends, and about the processes that a social worker must follow. So, the presumption that you cannot be confident that the outcome is right if you fail to follow a fair process is one that is entirely consistent with certain ethical frameworks (in particular deontological ethics) as well as the law. Social workers who manipulate processes in order to achieve the ends that they have predetermined to be right are likely to find themselves subject to strident criticism within judicial review or other legal challenges. On the other hand, we are talking about legal processes here not as a procedural straitjacket, nor a tick-box exercise, but as a disciplined approach to fair dealing.

That is not to say that the law cannot from time to time effectively construct a procedural manual that social workers have to follow. The Care Planning, Placement and Case Review (England) Regulations 2010, for example, are highly prescriptive in relation to the content of the process of care planning, and the nature and frequency of case reviews, in relation to Looked After Children.

Nor is it only legislation that can provide social workers with prescriptive procedural rules. Section 20 of the Children Act sets out on its face a procedure for social workers to work with children and families without judicial oversight. In practice, following criticism of abuse of that process, caselaw has prescribed very detailed prerequisites for how the power to accommodate is exercised, down to the level of detail of prescribing information that must be contained within the written agreement that the legislation itself does not even refer to. In relation to adults, detailed procedures in relation to deprivations of liberty have been constructed purely through caselaw, in a series of cases known colloquially, though not very informatively, as the Re X procedures (see for example X (Court of Protection Practice), Re [2015] EWCA Civ 599 (16 June 2015)).

Task 5.4 Task for students and practice educators

An earlier task invited the student to consider a form of intervention they might creatively use with a service user. Revisit that task or consider another.

Did you devise the intervention in order to achieve a particular goal, or did you devise the intervention in order to answer a particular question? Whether the end was predetermined says something about both your ethical approach and your legal approach – in respect of the latter, it might indicate whether you perceive the law as a tool or a manual. What do you think it says? Do you think that changing focus between means and ends would have made any difference to your work with the service user? Why?

Conclusion: Three questions to model an integrated approach to legal thinking

The placement experience represents both a mandatory and a formative part of social work's professional training, and practice educators have a central role within that. If law is 'othered' within the practice component of training, by suggesting that legal questions are the province of another profession, beyond the grasp of the social worker, or alien to their professional values, the law is likely to be viewed unconstructively as a weapon or barrier. Critical engagement embraces the law as a tool or manual to achieve social work's objects, even while being alert to its inherent contradictions and its flaws. While I have highlighted both of these, I propose a model to integrate critical thinking about the law with its constructive use in practice.

The essential characteristic of this model is that the necessary questions and reflections offered up by thinking about ethics and values, policies and agency practices, research and resource indicators, and other non-legal issues are sandwiched between the two questions that the law and legal thinking are authoritatively placed to answer: namely, whether a proposed course of action is lawful, and whether a proposed course of action is mandatory.

Thus, questions are first asked to determine what the service user wants, or would agree to, whether this is constrained by the rights of others or the absence of an illegally permissive framework, etc. A conclusion that you can proceed at this stage indicates only that it is lawful to do so, not that it is indicated. Non-legal considerations come into play prior to forming a final conclusion on the chosen course of action. The three stages, and the questions asked at each of those three stages may be represented as shown in Table 5.5.

Task 5.5 Task for students

Use the 'Can I? Should I? Must I?' approach set out in Table 5.5 to review a piece of work being considered for portfolio presentation. By considering all of the questions in the second column, what is your short answer to the questions in the first column? Reflect on whether you should change anything in relation to the work you are undertaking, or how you present it.

Table 5.5 Reflective questions for the 'Can I? Should I? Must I?' approach

Can I?	Is the intervention requested by the service user?
	Is the intervention wanted by the service user?
	Can I secure informed consent to the intervention?
	Is there any prohibition on my intervening in this way?
	Do the conflicting wishes/powers/duties of others point against the intervention?
Should I?	Is the intervention consistent with anti-oppressive and anti-discriminatory practice?
	Is the intervention ethical?
	Is the intervention efficacious?
	Are resources available to support the intervention?
	Is the intervention contra-indicated by the rights of/interests of/risk to others?
Must I?	Am I under a legal duty?
	What is my assessment of proportionality and risk?
	Have I reviewed the available alternatives?
	Is this consistent with the legal rights of the service user?

References

Ball, C, Harris, R, Roberts, G and Vernon, S (1988) *The Law Report: Teaching and Assessment of Law in Social Work Education.* London: CCETSW.

Bilson, A (2018) Policies on Bruises in Premobile Children: Why We Need Improved Standards for Policymaking. *Child & Family Social Work*, 1–8. https://doi.org/10.1111/cfs.12463

Braye, S and Preston-Shoot, M (2005) *Teaching, Learning and Assessment of Law in Social Work Education.* London: SCIE.

CCETSW (Central Council for Education and Training in Social Work) (1995) *Assuring Quality in the Diploma in Social Work: Rules and Requirements for the DipSW.* London: CCETSW.

College of Social Work (nd) *Professional Capabilities Framework* [online] Available at: www.basw.co.uk/pcf/capabilities/?level=8&domain=4#start (accessed 2 May 2018).

HCPC (Health and Care Professions Council) (2017) *Standards of Proficiency for Social Workers in England.* London: HCPC.

Healy, L M (2008) Exploring the History of Social Work as a Human Rights Profession. *International Social Work*, 51(6): 735–48.

Humphries, B (2004) An Unacceptable Role for Social Work: Implementing Immigration Policy. *British Journal of Social Work*, 34(1): 93–107.

Ife, J (2001) Local and Global Practice: Relocating Social Work as a Human Rights Profession in the New Global Order. *European Journal of Social Work*, 4(1): 5–15.

Ife, J (2012) *Human Rights and Social Work* (3rd ed). Cambridge: Cambridge University Press.

International Federation of Social Workers (IFSW) (2000) *Definition of Social Work Adopted by the IFSW General Meeting in Montréal, Canada*. [online] Available at: https://web.archive.org/web/20120720060835/http://ifsw.org/policies/definition-of-social-work (accessed 2 May 2018).

International Federation of Social Workers (IFSW) (2014) *Global Definition of Social Work*. [online] Available at: http://ifsw.org/policies/definition-of-social-work (accessed 2 May 2018).

Rodriguez-Blanco, V (2014) *Law and Authority under the Guise of the Good*. Oxford: Hart Publishing.

TSol (Treasury Solicitors) (2006) *The Judge Over Your Shoulder* (4th ed). London: TSol.

Twining, W (1967) Pericles and the Plumber. *Law Quarterly Review*, 83: 396–426.

United Nations (1994) *Human Rights and Social Work: A Manual for Schools of Social Work and the Social Work Profession* Geneva, Switzerland: United Nations Centre for Human Rights.

Chapter 6

Anti-oppressive practice, social work values and ethics

Sue Hollinrake

Introduction

A fundamental aspect of social work practice is the professional value base which, together with skills and knowledge, comprises the social work professional's 'toolbox'; the relationship between these three will be discussed in this chapter. Practice learners need to recognise how their practice, in which they apply their knowledge and skills, is guided and underpinned by professional values, and to appreciate the dilemmas, tensions and conflicts that can arise in their application. They are expected to be able to demonstrate their application of professional values in accounts of their practice in order to demonstrate their growing competence and capability, both for the benefit of service users and also for assessment purposes. This chapter will point learners to the ways in which they can appreciate, demonstrate and evidence their awareness of values for the development of confident and ethical practice. The discussion that follows will consider important aspects of learning from the pre-placement phase of preparing for practice through to the final placement phase where learners are becoming more independent.

Initially, practice learners are closely guided through the judgements and decisions they have to make by their practice educators, and they learn to work reflexively and to make use of supervision to explore the complexities of ethical decision-making, as they become more independent learners. Reflective journals and recordings of discussions in supervision are important tools for practice learners in this process for developing their self-awareness and reflexivity in order to become more confident in their practice, as they move towards qualification and registration as social workers. The significance of these tools for learning and developing will be discussed further below.

This chapter will also explore the nature, historical evolution and application of values to social work practice. In examining these different aspects, it will also demonstrate to the practice learner how values and anti-oppressive practice can be integrated into their practice learning, and how dilemmas and conflicts, the management of which can feel daunting at times, can be recognised and worked through, providing opportunities for growth and development.

What are values?

Firstly, in the process of preparing for practice placement, it is important to tease out what values are and why they are an important element in professional social work practice. Values are different from, but work alongside, facts. Facts encompass knowledge about laws, policies and procedures, theories, methods, networks and communities, which Howe (2014, p 153) explains as factual knowledge (knowing *that*) that a professional needs to know to be able to do her job. He identifies the other kind of knowledge that social workers need as knowledge *how*, that is, skills and techniques that have to be practised to become a skilled and competent practitioner. But as Howe (2014, pp 154–5) points out, neither facts nor skills without values make for competent practice:

Knowledge of facts and 'knowing that' on their own would not define a competent social worker. It is what is done with the factual knowledge – laws, procedures, theories, methods – that matters ... knowing how to do something and being skillful at doing it still does not say whether it should be done in the first place. Deciding whether a thing should be done involves making a judgement and making judgements involves values.

Howe's point emphasises the centrality of values in practice. Banks (2012, p 7) describes values as *'particular types of belief that people hold about what is regarded as worthy or valuable'*. Other associated words are principles, attitudes, opinions or preferences but generally values are stronger than attitudes, opinions or preferences, and linked more to ethics and morals, in terms of what is the right thing to do, which is then often described in terms of principles that guide actions, and conveyed in terms of what 'ought to be done' (whether or not it is done is then a moral choice). As Thompson (2015, p 125) states, *'At its simplest, a value is something we hold dear, something we see as important and worthy of safeguarding.'*

A value, then, in general terms, is about worth and desirability, whether we are referring to an object, for example, a diamond ring that has been given a value of £2000 to denote its desirability in relation to other rings and their values, or a friendship that we value or deem to be worth keeping and promoting. In either case, we make a choice. In the case of the ring, the choice is about affordability and whether we think a particular ring is worth the value placed on it by the seller, or, in the case of a friendship, we may think about why we might consider this one beneficial and prefer it to another.

We learn about what is valuable in life from others in our networks, through socialisation into our particular family and culture. Specific values are communicated to us through the actions of others and we adopt them as our own, through the social institutions of family, school, religion and work. The media also expresses dominant social values and we hear terms through the media such as 'shared values', 'British values', 'liberal values' and 'the value of free speech'.

Such expressions point to the significance of 'value systems' within a given culture, in which the importance of dominant values, as organised into a belief system, is frequently stressed through the media, politics, religion and other institutions to signify the preferred choices of behaviour for citizens – such as in Western-style capitalist economies where personal freedom, independence and choice are valued. In other societies, different values may be stressed and communicated through social institutions, such as loyalty to the family or social group and religious observance. As we grow and develop a sense of who we are, then we may consciously adopt or reject the values we have been exposed to. Youth cultures notably often reject some of the values of their parents' generation.

In this sense, values contribute significantly to our identity and our sense of ourselves as individuals with our own personal moral codes, and as belonging to groups with shared values. It is commonly acknowledged that our personal values are often taken for granted and we may not be particularly aware of them (Thompson, 2015, p 125) but choose to act in certain ways, based on our values, out of habit or out of a vague notion about what we deem valuable in life – for example, that we enjoy meeting people from many different backgrounds and therefore value diversity without explicitly acknowledging this. Nonetheless, this serves to indicate to ourselves and to others that we attach importance to something through our actions. So our values guide and inform our actions, consciously and unconsciously, suggesting what we should do in a given situation (whether we do do it or not). But the more conscious we are of our values, then the more likely we are to behave consistently and in accordance with them, rather than just pay lip service to them. In this way, we can see that values are both abstract and general (for example, valuing the dignity and worth of all human life) and practical and specific (for example, social workers, when undertaking assessments, must respect the views of individual service users and work collaboratively). These different characteristics will be returned to later when looking at the philosophical roots of ethical decision-making.

There are numerous ways through which we acquire values, such as:

- » modelling behaviour and absorbing attitudes and beliefs from our family, social and religious upbringing;
- » conforming to rules and regulations – for example, expected behaviour in social situations such as school;

>> listening to speakers who inspire us as they express their values and we are encouraged to adopt their values, or their passion reinforces our values and beliefs;

>> reading about issues and being convinced through discussion and reflection on our own values, which may cause us to change or revise them.

Our own personal values – how we acquire them and how we work with them in practice

It is important for practice learners, in preparing for practice placement, to identify their personal values, as they must have awareness and knowledge of their own values in order to understand how these might influence the judgements they make in practice, alongside what their professional knowledge and skills, and their employing organisation, might be suggesting they ought to do.

Task 6.1

Think about your own personal values.

Make a list of the six most important ones.

Make some notes about how you acquired them and where they came from.

How does this list accord with what you already know about the social work professional value base and where do you experience tensions or difficulties?

Note – for those practice learners whose cultural background differs from the prevailing culture in which they are undertaking their social work education, then it is important to be aware of any differences in attitudes and values and to explore the impact the interactions between the different sets of values has on you as a learner. You might want to think about this in relation to the next task.

Task 6.2

This exercise is useful for tuning in (see Taylor and Devine, 1993, pp 20–2) to service users' situations before meeting them to conduct an assessment and can be used as part of a reflective log for preparation for practice learning.

Think about a service user – an elderly man who requires support at home in order to be discharged from hospital after a fall. Think about how this elderly man may be feeling at the prospect of going back home. Imagine you are in his shoes.

How would you like to be treated? What would you expect in a social worker's behaviour towards you? Make a list of your expectations. This may help in enabling you to have an open mind to listen to the service user.

How does your list of statements compare with your own personal values, considered in Task 6.1?

Note – service users tend to value social workers for their ability to listen, to be 'in relationship' with them, to be empathic, responsive to individual preferences, paying attention to issues they see as important, and to be honest and clear about what they can and cannot do (Carr, 2004; Doel and Best, 2008; Gosling and Martin, 2012).

Strategies for managing value conflicts in practice

It is not unusual for social work students to feel that their personal values are being challenged either through university-based learning or when they go out on placement, working with service users or with other professionals. As practice learners, students will be exposed to new experiences and perspectives on life that are different from their own. Attitudes and values that they have unquestioningly accepted suddenly come under scrutiny. Challenges are inevitable and these can be significant and even life changing. For students on practice placement, it is important that personal values are thought about (for example, in reflective logs and in supervision) and clarified, through a process referred to as *value clarification* (see Higham (2006), Chapter 5), which is part of increasing one's self-awareness. The use of a reflective log is important in this process, to self-monitor, to question and to consider different value positions so that personal influences can be thought about through internal reflection and shared in supervision in order to engage with the tensions in practice that inevitably arise and which have to be ethically managed. Supervision should provide a safe environment and a trusting relationship in which there is space to explore these differences. As Beckett and Maynard (2013, p 11) highlight, personal values influence why a person chooses social work as their profession, and they cannot always be separated from professional values, but if this is the case, then a high degree of self-awareness is required, which students will start to develop, so that, as Banks (2012, p 176) states, *'where they conflict, the social worker as a person has a moral responsibility to decide which has primacy and to justify this decision'.*

Professional values

According to Higham (2006), at their core, social work values involve:

- » showing respect for persons;
- » intervening appropriately to protect vulnerable individuals;
- » promoting their quality of life;
- » honouring the diverse and distinctive organisations and communities that make up contemporary society;
- » combatting processes that lead to discrimination, marginalisation and social exclusion;
- » empowering and emancipating individuals, groups and communities.

Much of the recent literature on social work values (for example, Banks, 2012; Beckett and Maynard, 2013; Bell and Hafford-Letchfield, 2015; Thompson, 2015) groups together the individual values into two streams. Typically, the 'traditional' stream focuses on the values applicable to work with individuals, deriving from the Judeo-Christian tradition in social work and developed within social work by key writers such as Biestek (1961), Butrym (1976) and Timms (1983). This stream emphasises the worth of each individual human being and their right to respect, acceptance, non-judgementalism and self-determination, connecting with Rogerian person-centred values (Rogers, 1951).

Taking on a more political perspective, the second stream, that of 'emancipatory' values, focuses on a commitment to social justice through the application of anti-discriminatory and anti-oppressive practice, which acknowledge the socio-political aspects of people's lives, and seek to promote a rights-based and a strengths-based approach through empowerment and collaboration with service users and carers. An appreciation of the impact on individuals of discrimination and oppression is funda-mental to anti-discriminatory and anti-oppressive practice, as is the significance of recognising and celebrating diversity. In this respect, practice learners are working towards an understanding that diversity characterises and shapes human experience and is critical to the formation of identity. Diversity is multi-dimensional and includes ethnicity, disability, class, economic status, age, sexuality, gender and transgender status, faith and belief. To become competent social workers, practice learners need to appreciate that, as a consequence of difference, a person's life experience may include discrimination, oppression, marginalisation and alienation and they need to learn to challenge appropriately. Once these concepts have been understood, then practice learners will also acquire and develop the knowledge and skills required to become culturally competent, as discussed below.

But, first of all, prior to undertaking a practice placement, it is important to be aware of the difference between discrimination and oppression and the similarities between these two concepts, and to be aware of personal experiences of these.

Task 6.3

Take a few moments to think about discrimination and what it means to you. What experiences have you had of being discriminated against? How do/did you feel about these experiences. Write down a list of words you associate with the term 'discrimination'.

You might have the following in your list:

Unequal

Unfair

Disrespectful

Offensive

Unlawful

Hurtful

Threatening

Prejudice

Persecution

These words describe negative experiences or feelings. Discrimination, however, means simply to identify a difference, as Thompson notes (2012, p 12), and we do this in our lives everyday, in distinguishing differences between things and people in our environment. In order to value the uniqueness of an individual service user, a social worker must distinguish a whole range of characteristics and experiences belonging to that particular person, in order to appreciate their needs and to ensure an accurate assessment. However, the negative expression of discrimination, by which some people are *discriminatory* towards others, usually as members of particular groups of people in society, has a damaging effect as the following definition highlights:

Unjust or prejudicial treatment of a person or group, especially on the grounds of race, gender, sexual orientation, etc.; frequently with against. *Also (with* in favour of*): favourable treatment of a person or group, in order to compensate for disadvantage or lack of privilege.*

(Oxford Dictionaries, 2015)

As this definition highlights, the negative effects of discrimination can be countered by 'positive discrimination' but this must conform to the conditions for 'positive action' as outlined in the Equality Act 2010.

Power is an important element of both discrimination and oppression and as social workers exercise power then the implications of its use and misuse (for example, through the unconscious privileging of some service users because of the resonance with one's own experiences of discrimination) need to be understood and considered by the practice learner in their accounts of their practice. Oppression takes the process of the misuse of power a step further through the addition of institutional power, whereby groups of people become marginalised, excluded and disadvantaged because of the political and social contexts that promote inequality and perpetuate the negative attitudes and responses of wider society. Oppression is usually maintained through an ideology of superiority, which is utilised to manage human differences through simplistic oppositions – superior and inferior, which de Beauvoir (1949, p 24), a French feminist writer, explained as follows:

One of the benefits that oppression confers upon the oppressors is that the most humble among them is made to <u>feel</u> superior.

Oppression also conveys the shared nature of experiences that result from being on the receiving end of different forms of discrimination, based within the power that others wield against groups that have become marginalised. Audrey Lorde, a Black feminist, discussed the impact of the institutionalised management of difference, linking this to the economic relationships in which some groups profit from the oppression of other groups:

Institutionalized rejection of difference is an absolute necessity in a profit economy which needs outsiders as surplus people. As members of such an economy, we have all been programmed to respond to the human differences between us with fear and loathing and to handle that difference in one of three ways: ignore it, and if that is not possible, copy it if we think it is dominant, or destroy it if we think it is subordinate. But we have no patterns for relating across our human differences as equals. As a result, those differences have been misnamed and misused in the service of separation and confusion.

(Lorde, 1984, p 115)

Thompson, in his seminal work on anti-discriminatory practice, produced the PCS model (Thompson, 2012, p 26), which is a very useful tool to use to think in depth about the impact of discrimination and oppression on individual service users, and to understand how they are affected by wider social forces that maintain negative constructions about difference as expressed through prejudice, discrimination and oppression. Discrimination and oppression are experienced within and across one or more different social divisions – class, ethnicity, gender, sexual orientation, disability, age – and a number of processes reinforce the negative experiences of marginalised groups:

» stigmatisation (something that marks out a person as unworthy and discredits them);

» prejudice (a learned attitude linked to a stereotype and often based on bias and intolerance);

» infantilisation (attributing a disempowering child-like status that can restrict rights and citizenship);

» stereotyping (the misinformed perception that certain groups share distinguishing characteristics based on assumptions and generalisations).

In his tripartite model, Thompson created a simple diagram with three concentric circles. The inner point of the first circle is labelled 'P' to denote the personal level which refers to the level of personal prejudice, the use of negative language to describe difference and diversity, and the impact on the individual service user's psychological level of experience – their beliefs, ideas and perceptions, where the experience of discrimination and oppression can lead to 'internalised oppression'. This is the process through which the individual concerned can internalise the negative beliefs of the dominant ideology and experience low self-esteem, poor self-image and self-efficacy as a result. Black people in a 'white world', women in a male-dominated environment, disabled people in surroundings designed for the able-bodied can all experience physical and psychological barriers to their own progress as a result of the unjust exercise of power. It is a mutually reinforcing process in which a sense of their own lack of advantage is then individualised because the outside world does not accept or acknowledge that this disadvantage exists and so they come to accept the inaccurate myths and stereotypes about their group. The next two circles, moving outwards, are 'C' (culture, community and conformity – the level of shared values) and 'S' (structural, societal, socio-political – the level at which beliefs are cemented by, for example, the media, religion and government policy, and through which levels of disadvantage and social inequality can be acutely and chronically experienced with very damaging effects – for example, poor housing, low income, high unemployment, high crime levels in the neighbourhood). The inter-relatedness of all three levels helps students to think about their cumulative effect on the life of the service user and to locate the negative forces of discrimination and oppression, which they experience personally within their local community and wider society. This model can be very useful in 'tuning in' to service users' situations, as in Task 6.2 above. Such an analysis can then be coupled with a strengths-based approach to empower the service user to make changes and encourage a more self-determining attitude.

Task 6.4

This exercise helps you to think about the way in which difference is managed through the negative use of power.

Look up two poems by Benjamin Zephaniah – (can be accessed on YouTube) 'The Death of Joy Gardner'

www.youtube.com/watch?v=5UX7QapfZuU

and 'White Comedy'

www.youtube.com/watch?v=K_bPVkAWUQw

These poems illustrate how discrimination (in this case racial discrimination) can take many forms – behaviour or words – subtle or violent. This extends to all forms of discrimination. Think about this in relation to another dimension – for example, age, disability, gender or sexual orientation – and write down some ways in which behaviour or words are used to discriminate. Maybe you know of a poem that expresses this in relation to another disadvantaged group.

Now think about a service user that you have worked with in practice and consider the various ways in which he or she has experienced different forms of discrimination (through words and behaviours) and across different dimensions (class, ethnicity, gender and so on, referred it as intersectionality). Think about the impact of prejudice, discrimination and oppression on this service user. Try to *get in their shoes'* and *'tune in'* (Taylor and Devine, 1993, pp 20–2) to how these experiences feel for them and how they affect their lives.

Students then need to take further this understanding of discrimination and oppression, to think about how to work on placement in an anti-discriminatory and anti-oppressive way, which is fundamental to competent social work practice. This seeks to identify discrimination and oppression, through using a tool like the PCS model discussed above, to understand its origins and impact, with the aim of combatting it to promote social justice, improved well-being and better outcomes for service users. In addition to recognising and challenging discrimination and oppression, practice learners must also develop knowledge and skills in what has been termed cultural competence (see Tedam, in Bartoli, 2013, pp 48–65 for a detailed discussion). It is an important component of good practice to recognise diversity as normative and respond to difference positively, as a way of showing respect for individual service users and their families and communities, through gaining knowledge and appreciation of different cultures, as well as an awareness of one's own culture in relation to other cultures. This means working in a reflexive manner (Taylor and White, 2000), listening carefully to oneself, and to the personal narrative of the service user. It means appreciating how individuals see themselves and their own identity, seeing diverse identities as equal to one another and not privileging one over another, and how a particular narrative is situated in wider contexts and may change with time and place, in which different aspects of identity such as age, ethnicity, gender and culture may shift in significance according to circumstance. Consideration of the different roles, identities and narratives of both the practitioner and service user, how they interplay and impact on each other, along with recognition of commonalities and differences, are key to practising anti-oppressively (Clifford and Burke, 2009). Dominelli (2009, p 53) refers to anti-oppressive practice as transformational practice because of the different levels on which it works.

Task 6.5

When on placement, the use of a *critical incident exercise* (see Green Lister, 2012, pp 107–19) in supervision with a practice educator can be a useful tool to think about how practising in an anti-discriminatory manner can empower a service user. For this, the practice learner brings a case to supervision that they have recently worked on and which has challenged their beliefs and values in a significant way. Firstly the practice learner sets the context by describing the service user(s), their situation and the concerns/issues that require change. Then they describe the incident or encounter – what happened, what they did, who else was involved, what they did and what the outcomes were. Then the practice learner reflects on why this happened; was it an atypical occurrence/interaction or maybe part of an emerging pattern of interaction? How were their beliefs and values challenged? In particular, they should think about the dimensions of difference involved (class, ethnicity, gender etc). How did these affect the relationship between practice learner and the service user? How were power differences managed? How did the practice learner feel during and after the event? They should then think about the standpoints of the others involved – what might they have been thinking and feeling? What are the different theories of understanding (psychological and sociological) that might explain and make sense of what happened? What are the different value perspectives and the different theories for intervention that promote anti-discriminatory practice and how could these be used to engage the service user collaboratively and promote empowerment? What can the practice learner identify as new learning in terms of values, skills and knowledge that has been gained from this exercise and how might it be transferred into practice?

Two or three streams of values – separate or connected?

The two streams discussed so far, traditional and emancipatory, are not separate entities that are unrelated. In effect they work together, helping to see the individual in context and are linked, in particular, through the pivotal value of 'respect for persons' which bridges the two streams. Person-centred values can be applied in work in an individual way with service users and carers, while emancipatory values acknowledge the need to understand and work effectively with that particular person in context, to understand and combat the impact of structural pressures and omissions. Whittington and Whittington (2015, p 82) propose a third stream – that of 'governance' – which incorporates organisational values and practices arising from managerialist approaches within service organisation and delivery which emphasise the service user as consumer exercising choice and control, and organisations committed to efficiency, effectiveness and economy (value for money).

Task 6.6

From your experiences on practice, see if you can find an example of the disconnection between agency policy statements and its priorities in practice. Think about the conflict or dilemma this may pose for you as a practice learner.

How to evidence these streams of values in your accounts of practice

To present a case study, briefly describe the incident or issue from practice that forms your case study and consider the following:

» What relevant legislation applies and what are the underpinning, assumed principles from this legislation that impact on how you discharge your role?

» What skills did you require to promote these values? Think particularly about how your communication skills supported the promotion of your professional values (see for example Parris, 2012, Section 3).

» What were the traditional and emancipatory values that you were utilising in your interaction with the service user(s), and what skills did you use to ensure you communicated these (for example, person-centred skills to ensure respect for persons and self-determination and empathy to convey an understanding of the impact of discrimination and oppression arising from difference)?

» What other knowledge was important that informed your perspective – for example, in relation to emancipatory values, what sociological issues would be relevant (consider, for example, explanations about poverty, or an understanding of social divisions). How did power and powerlessness impact upon the interaction between yourself, the service user and the organisation within which you were/are working. How can you critically apply this knowledge to your case study?

Note: You will see from the approach suggested here that there is an important inter-play, as explained earlier, between values, knowledge and skills.

Historical development of the professional value base

The professional value base has been gradually established over many years and through different sources of influence. To understand how and why the value base of social work has developed, it is helpful to look at its historical development. In Britain (and in other countries where social work developed), the legacy of religious ideals is apparent, through the help provided by the Christian Church for those in need from medieval times through to the nineteenth-century charitable organisations, which provided support and financial help to the poor. These institutions, alongside other religiously based ones, such as Jewish charitable organisations, infused the value base of the social work profession as it emerged in the twentieth century, with values about human dignity and worth, the uniqueness of individuals, acceptance of and respect for persons and being non-condemnatory and respectful in dealings with others.

Another significant influence came in the early 1960s, when social work embraced theory and values from the newly emerging humanistic psychology and psychotherapy of Maslow and Rogers, which through the writings of Biestek, a Catholic priest, brought a refinement and expansion of these traditional values (Biestek, 1961) with his list of instrumental values in his seven casework principles (acceptance, having a non-judgemental attitude, individualisation, the purposeful expression of feeling, confidentiality, self-determination and controlled emotional involvement). During the 1960s and 1970s, other theorists (Pearson, 1975; Butrym, 1976; Timms, 1983) adopted modified versions of Biestek's list of principles, often with the addition of the ultimate or basic principle of 'respect for persons'. A key theme running through all these principles could be identified as: *respect for the individual person as a self-determining being*.

Merging traditional and emancipatory values, more recently, Sarah Banks (2012, p 60) proposed three basic first-order principles as relevant to social work; respect for the dignity and worth of all human beings; the promotion of welfare or well-being; and the promotion of social justice. Respect for persons is the core value that underpins all interactions between social workers and service users and carers. This links to non-judgementalism – ie a social worker may be required to make judgements about an individual service user's behaviour or circumstances, but will avoid judging the individual as a person, deeming them worthy of respect and valuing their uniqueness as an individual, irrespective of their behaviour and actions. This is not always as easy and straightforward as it initially sounds, as the following task highlights.

Task 6.7 Task for students

Can you think of a situation in practice where you might find it difficult to remain respectful towards a service user because of your own personal values/experiences?

How might you manage such a conflict in practice? What strategies would you need to employ to ensure you were professional at all times (look back at an earlier section of this chapter on *Strategies for managing value conflicts in practice* and illustrate from your own experience)?

How might you write about this in a way that evidences self-awareness and reflection?

The role of regulatory bodies in the development of the professional value base

Organisations representing professional social work have had a role in constructing professional values for practitioners and making statements about how professionals are expected to adhere to a set of common values. As in other professions like medicine and law, regulatory bodies such as the current one for social work, the Health and Care Professions Council (soon to be changed to Social Work England), produce codes of practice and conduct which embody the profession's core values and to which professionals are expected to adhere. Professional organisations for which membership is optional also produce codes of ethics. The most recent codes of ethics are from the (former) College of Social Work (TCSW) (it closed in 2015), which produced a Code of Ethics in 2013 (TCSW, 2013) and from the British Association of Social Work (BASW), which revised its Code of Ethics in 2014 (BASW, 2014). When joining their profession or a professional organisation, social workers agree to work to these rules or codes of conduct which provide guidance on how, as a student or qualified professional, they should behave towards others such as service users and their carers, or other professionals.

An appreciation of the shifts in these codes provides an understanding of how and why these have changed in emphasis over time. A notable example concerns the Central Council for the Education and Training of Social Workers (CCETSW), set up in 1974, which, in 1989, produced a statement (Paper 30) (CCETSW, 1989) about the requirements of the Diploma in Social Work (DipSW) with an annex, authored by its Black Perspectives Committee, which focused on its position on racism that DipSW programmes, introduced in the UK in 1989, were expected to reflect. As stated by Bamford (2015, p 97), this was ahead of its time, as it claimed that major institutions in British society were institutionally racist. However, the ensuing political backlash from the government of the time and the media forced the production of a Revised Paper 30 (CCETSW, 1995) with a removal of Annex 5 and a watering down of language, moving away from anti-racism and anti-discrimination to combat endemic racism, to references to equal opportunities and the valuing of difference, which fail to recognise structural causes of exclusion and deprivation.

Importantly, this episode illustrates the impact of differing political perspectives and associated values on the profession. CCETSW was accused of political correctness and was replaced in 2001 by the General Social Care Council. The GSCC produced two codes of practice – one for social care workers and one for their employers. In both cases, these were a list of standards for professional conduct and practice. With the demise of the GSCC in 2012, the regulation and professional organisation for social work was split between the Health and Care Professions Council (HCPC), which is the regulatory body, and The College of Social Work, set up to promote standards within the social work profession. The College closed in July 2015 and BASW has taken over its PCF. In summary, the different codes and statements which currently exist and encompass and express the professional value base are as follows:

» HCPC Standards of Conduct, Performance and Ethics (for registrants) (2012a)

» HCPC Guidance on Conduct and Ethics for Students (2012b)

» The Professional Capabilities Framework (The College of Social Work, 2012b) (now managed and delivered by BASW)

» British Association of Social Workers (BASW) Revised Code of Ethics (2014)

» International Federation of Social Workers (IFSW) – Ethics in Social Work – Statement of Principles (2012)

Task 6.8

Have a look at these different codes. Compare and contrast. What do they have in common and what differences do you notice? What kind of information do they contain?

Comment: Codes of practice tend to be made up of principles, to be generally applied, or rules, which usually have a more specific application. They tend to state the core purpose of the profession; may include some character traits expected (for example, being honest and trustworthy); broad value statements for the profession – for example, respect for individuals, upholding human dignity and worth; general statements about the aims of professional practice – for example, working in partnership, working collaboratively; and specific rules for practice – for example, HCPC Standards of Conduct, Performance and Ethics, Standard 10, 'You must keep accurate records' (HCPC, 2012a).

The Professional Capabilities Framework

Embedded throughout the Professional Capabilities Framework (PCF) for Social Workers in England introduced by The College of Social Work in 2012 and now hosted and updated by BASW (2018) are aspects of values that as a student you need to become familiar with to ensure that you are practising to the required standard and can extrapolate from practice relevant elements for discussion and analysis to evidence how you have performed against the requirements of the PCF. The updated PCF has integrated the BASW Code of Ethics where professional guidance on ethics is referenced, and has also placed emphasis on person-centred practice and on acting to promote human rights (BASW, 2018, p 3). The expectations for the different levels of competence (Entry, Readiness for direct practice, End of first placement, End of last placement/completion etc) change and increase as the student progresses through to qualification and beyond. For example, Domain 2 is entitled Values and ethics, and this refers to the knowledge and understanding that a social worker must have about the range of professional values, about the impact of their own personal values on professional relationships and the required competence in making ethical decisions in practice (which you will need to illustrate in accounts of your practice), while Domain 3 focuses on Diversity, and requires that social workers understand and respect difference and diversity and practice in a culturally competent manner. Domain 4 (Rights, justice and economic well-being) emphasises the fundamental principles of human rights, social justice and economic well-being as enshrined in national and international laws, and conventions to promote equality through empowerment and advocacy, and Domain 5 (Knowledge) encompasses a range of knowledge relevant to practice that relates to professional ethics and values through a critical appreciation of the psychological and sociological theories that inform our understanding of the impact of injustice, discrimination and oppression and how we then use these to critically reflect on and analyse our practice (Domain 6) to promote change and positive outcomes for service users. Values are expressed in relationship through skills and interventions so Domain 7 is also a crucial area of practice linked to the professional value base, as is Domain 8, Contexts and organisations, which emphasises the social worker's responsibility to work to the values to their employing organisation. As social workers practice within and across organisations, then the impact of organisations on practice through either promoting or undermining professional values and ethical practice has to be considered along with any conflicts and dilemmas that may occur, so Domain 8 is also important here. Finally, Professional leadership, Domain 9, has to be considered too as, for example, making good use of quality supervision to reflect on practice and ensure sound decision-making is important for practice learners and qualified practitioners within a management structure that promotes continuing professional development and fosters leadership skills that enhance the education and development of others. It is important that throughout your writing and reflection on your practice that you refer to these domains as they apply to your practice and critically reflect on how you have met these capabilities.

Value sources and their interaction

As discussed above, it is important for practice learners to develop an awareness of personal values and how they interact with the professional value base. Societal values or moral codes impact on personal values and influence professional codes and agency/organisational values as well. The values underpinning legislation and policy are another value source, which have an impact on the values of social care organisations and the responsibilities and duties of social workers. This array of different sources of values in professional practice can produce a complex mix of expectations with potential tensions and conflicts about moral choices in deciding which particular value source should take precedence and why. An example of this is the policy development of personalisation in adult social care, which promotes individual rights, choice and control, and equal partnerships (co-production) between service users and social care organisations (SCIE, 2010, 2015). However, in times of austerity, when the burden of financial constraints on local authorities has a real impact on resources and personal funding for support, then tensions arise in practice between the exercising of two different policy initiatives.

Task 6.9

Think of an example from your practice placement of a tension or conflict between different values arising from different sources and reflect on how you managed the tension/conflict and what strategies you used to access the support that you needed to resolve the tension/conflict.

Social work values and ethical philosophy

Achieving a basic understanding of some key pillars of thinking in Western European ethical philosophy is helpful in making sense of elements of the professional value base of social work, and in particular in teasing out and managing conflicts and dilemmas that arise when two different moral positions converge within a practice context.

There are several different ethical frameworks that require some consideration as they have a bearing on everyday social work ethical decision-making. Beginning with *deontology*, the most important deontological moral philosopher is the Enlightenment thinker Immanuel Kant (1724–1804). His philosophy is based on the notion of universalism, that is, that for a moral choice and consequent action to be good then it must be applied equally to everyone. Thus, the test for a moral action for Kant was that it had to be applicable to everyone – hence his notion of the categorical imperative (that is, the statement has no qualifying factors or influencing variables – it is categorical, and there is an instruction to action – it is imperative). His moral philosophy is based on the human capacity for rationality and also encompasses the notion of 'duty' (deontology is derived from the Greek word for duty). His 'practical impera-tive' stresses the importance of treating others as one would want to be treated – as a moral subject capable of rational thought and not to be used as an object and a means to someone else's preferences or ends. The ethical principles which have informed social work's traditional value base are in the main deontological, because they refer to rights and duties/responsibilities, such as respect for persons, the right to informed consent, human rights generally and the duty that professional social workers have to promote these rights, in particular in relation to groups of marginalised people who have been excluded from society and denied opportunities.

A dilemma can occur, however, when managers in an organisation exert power over one's professional judgement based on rational consideration of an individual ser-vice user's situation, and use their power, based on organisational principles and gov-ernment policies, to ration resources for the greater good of the greatest number of people – that is, limiting expenditure on social care by rationing through prioritising only the most severe need, because the *consequences* of not doing so, ie meeting all levels of need, would plunge the nation into further debt and economic chaos, thus affecting many people. This could be challenged on the grounds that this approach means that the needs of some people are valued more than the needs of others. Such a challenge would derive from a deontological approach. This kind of argument allows the practice learner or practitioner to tease out one moral philosophical approach from another to understand the different moral approaches to an ethical problem and choices of action – a deontological one in which the rights of all are deemed as equally important and based on universal principles, or the *utilitarian* (a form of *consequen-tialism*) position that determines whether an action is right or wrong on the basis of its consequences, and its capacity to do more good overall than harm. The group of moral theories encompassing *consequentialism* and different forms of *utilitarianism* also developed during the Enlightenment period in Western Europe in the eighteenth century (thinkers such as David Hume [1711–1776], Jeremy Bentham [1748–1832] and later John Stuart Mill [1806–1873]).

Two quite different ethical frameworks from the two aforementioned are those of *virtue ethics* and the feminist *ethic of care*, which are approaches that are based on par-ticular and unique features of particular situations that are context-specific and rela-tive rather than universal in application. Virtue ethics is not based on outcomes or the consequences of moral decision-making, or on a moral duty and rule-following, but on the good qualities of an individual, in this case the social work practitioner or prac-tice learner. These are qualities that are virtuous and positive for the development of a good relationship with service users and which contribute to their well-being and to that of society as well. The Greek philosopher, Aristotle (384–323 BCE) was influential in developing this branch of moral philosophy and he saw the well-being of individuals as bound up with the well-being of society. Examples of relevant characteristics of practitioners that enable them to be good and effective in their roles are compassion and caring, kindness, honesty, integrity, wisdom (the ability to make good sound judgements), courage, being respectful, altruistic, fair-minded and benevolent. Such virtues, though, are not without their difficulties and conflicts in practice. For example, is it always wise to be honest, as in the case of a seriously ill person in hospital, when the multi-disciplinary team, including the social worker, make a decision not to be completely honest about their condition because being completely honest might do more harm (maleficence) at a particular point in their recovery than good (beneficence) and affect their overall progress? If such a decision to withhold some truth was applied, then this would be utilitarian because the consequence would justify the means.

While it is difficult to see how virtue ethics alone can help the practitioner to negotiate the complex and sometimes competing agendas in social care, as a guide to the desired character and personal qualities of the practitioner, particularly in relation to the concept of wisdom (the ability to make sound judgements), it provides the 'actors' (practitioners) with the right disposition to carry out the 'actions' which other ethical approaches might then determine. It should also be noted that service users value these qualities in practitioners and they support effective partnership working (Carr, 2004; Whittington and Whittington, 2015, pp 83–4).

The feminist ethic of care shares something in common with virtue ethics, in that it is concerned with the moral disposition of the person caring, which in this context would include the virtues described above, but in addition, it is a *practical* ethic, which is lodged in a specific set of circumstances and contextualised by a specific relationship. As such it demands attention to the skills necessary for caring relationships and the interactions between the carer and the cared-for person. This emphasis on disposition and character, *and* skills effectively links the ethic of care to relationship-based practice (Ruch et al, 2010).

Initially derived from the research of psychologist Carol Gilligan (1982), and developed as a philosophy by other writers such as Kittay (1999), Noddings (2003) and Tronto (1993), the ethic of care emerged in response to the perceived dominance of masculinist approaches to ethics that concentrate on rules, duties and rights. In the findings from her research into moral decision-making, Gilligan asserted that women tended to make moral judgements based on a concern to maintain relationships in an inclusive way, and she referred to this as a *'different voice'* from which an ethic of care then emerged. She linked it clearly to the *'activity of relationships, of seeing and responding to need, taking care of the world by sustaining the web of connection so that no one is left out'* (Gilligan, 1982, p 73).

Here she identified the situated judgements made often, but not exclusively, by women, based on connection with others, and she differentiated this approach to caring from the moral detachment based on reason and rules of conduct. Noddings (2003) located the origins of this approach in the private sphere of the family and child-rearing, and the sense of social responsibility experienced by women as a result of their socialisation into a female identity (a 'caring self' can be linked to virtue ethics), often but not exclusively undertaken by women. Noddings highlighted the significant features of receptivity, relatedness and responsiveness to the unique needs of the other cared-for individual, and also introduced the term 'engrossment' to describe the commitment that develops from the carer's personal connection and relatedness to the cared-for person, a dynamic particular to their situation (p 90).

Further work in this area highlights how interdependence and reciprocity are at the root of all human interactions. Tronto (1993) has identified four elements to an ethic of care – attentiveness, responsibility, competence and responsiveness. The first element refers to the moral disposition of recognising, understanding and caring about need in the cared-for person, and person-centred communication skills are clearly significant in achieving this; the second element refers to feeling a responsibility towards that person and being prepared to act with and for them (requiring skills in collaboration and advocacy); the third element requires the skills to be able to respond competently and effectively, which includes self-awareness and reflection; and the fourth element refers to enabling the cared-for person to be receptive to the care and be active in its delivery. It can be seen from these four elements how this ethic of care can be applied within relationships that are inter-dependent, encompassing both thinking and feeling with the application of emotional intelligence (Howe, 2008), and how it supports relationship-based practice and links well to social work's professional value base in relation to traditional values within one-to-one relationships. Further, in relation to anti-discriminatory practice, Held (2006) eloquently posits the concept of an ethic of care as a prerequisite for an ethic of justice, in that sensitivity to the needs of others at a one-to-one level can then develop into a wider concern for tackling injustice and inequality, and Orme (2002) has considered this in relation to social work practice.

Conclusion

This chapter has highlighted both the breadth and depth required from practice learners in their consideration of the application of the range of value perspectives that have to be taken into account to develop competent and capable practice. Breadth must be addressed in terms of demonstrating the various different sources of values

SUE HOLLINRAKE

that must be identified and understood, the two streams of professional values and their philosophical underpinnings. These then must be considered in the depth required when applying them in practice alongside the skills in relationship work, however brief the encounter with the service user or other professional(s) involved, because every encounter is unique and whether the focus of the work is on care or control, social justice should be the goal and outcome. In support of this, the care of the practice learner by the organisation, through supervision based on trust and transparency, should be the container that enables the learner to develop their reflexivity to ensure that the links between internal processes and the demands of the external world for both the practice learner and the service user can be made, understood and worked with.

References

Bamford, T (2015) *A Contemporary History of Social Work: Learning from the Past.* Bristol: Policy Press.

Banks, S (2012) *Ethics and Values in Social Work* (4th ed). Basingstoke: Palgrave Macmillan.

Beckett, C and Maynard, A (2013) *Values and Ethics in Social Work* (2nd ed). London: Sage.

Bell, L and Hafford-Letchfield, T (2015) *Ethics, Values and Social Work Practice.* Maidenhead: Open University Press.

Biestek, F (1961) *The Casework Relationship.* London: Allen and Unwin.

British Association of Social Workers (BASW) (2014) *Revised Code of Ethics.* [online] Available at: http://cdn.basw.co.uk/upload/basw_95243-9.pdf (accessed 23 June 2018).

British Association of Social Workers (BASW) (2018) *Professional Capabilities Framework for Social Workers in England. The 2018 Refreshed PCF.* [online] Available at: www.basw.co.uk/resources/professional-capabilitiesframework-social-work-england-0 (last accessed 7 July 2018).

Butrym, Z (1976) *The Nature of Social Work.* Basingstoke: Macmillan.

Carr, S (2004) *Has Service User Participation Made a Difference to Social Care Services?* SCIE Position Paper No. 3. London: Social Care Institute for Excellence.

Central Council for Education and Training in Social Work (CCETSW) (1989) *DipSW: Rules and Requirements for the Diploma in Social Work (Paper 30).* London: CCETSW.

Central Council for Education and Training in Social Work (CCETSW) (1995) *DipSW: Rules and Requirements for the Diploma in Social Work (Paper 30)* (revised ed). London: CCETSW.

Clifford, D and Burke, B (2009) *Anti-Oppressive Values and Ethics in Social Work.* Basingstoke: Palgrave Macmillan.

de Beauvoir, S (1949) *Introduction to The Second Sex.* Translated from French by Parshley, H M (1953). Harmondsworth: Penguin.

Doel, M and Best, L (2008) *Experiencing Social Work: Learning from Service Users.* London: Sage.

Dominelli, L (2009) Anti-Oppressive Practice: The Challenges of the Twenty-First Century, in Adams, R, Dominelli, L and Payne, M (eds) *Themes, Issues and Critical Debates* (3rd ed, pp 49–64). Basingstoke: Palgrave Macmillan.

Gilligan, C (1982) *In a Different Voice: Psychological Theory and Women's Development.* Cambridge, MA: Harvard University Press.

98

Gosling, J and Martin, J (2012) *Making Partnerships with Service Users and Advocacy Groups Work*. London: Jessica Kingsley.

Green Lister, P (2012) *Integrating Social Work Theory and Practice*. Abingdon: Routledge.

Health and Care Professions Council (HCPC) (2012a) *Standards of Conduct, Performance and Ethics*. London: HCPC. [online] Available at: www.hcpc-uk.org/assets/documents/10003B6EStandardsofconduct, performanceandethics.pdf (accessed 23 June 2018).

Health and Care Professions Council (HCPC) (2012b) *Guidance on Conduct and Ethics for Students*. London: HCPC. [online] Available at: www.hcpc-uk.org/assets/documents/10002D1BGuidanceonconduct andethicsforstudents.pdf (accessed 23 June 2018).

Held, V (2006) *The Ethics of Care: Personal, Political and Global*. Oxford, Oxford University Press.

Higham P (2006) *Social Work: Introducing Professional Practice*. London: Sage.

Howe, D (2008) *The Emotionally Intelligent Social Worker*. Houndsmill: Palgrave Macmillan.

Howe, D (2014) *The Complete Social Worker*. Basingstoke: Palgrave Macmillan.

International Federation of Social Workers (IFSW) (2012) *Ethics in Social Work – Statement of Principles*. [online] Available at: http://ifsw.org/policies/statement-of-ethical-principles (accessed 23 June 2018).

Kittay, E F (1999) *Love's Labor. Essays on Women, Equality, and Dependency*. New York: Routledge.

Lorde, A (1984) *Sister Outsider. Essays and Speeches by Audre Lorde*. Berkeley, CA: Crossing Press.

Noddings, N (2003) *Caring: A Feminine Approach to Ethics and Moral Education* (2nd ed). Berkeley, CA: University of California Press.

Orme, J (2002) Social Work: Gender, Care and Justice. *British Journal of Social Work*, 32(6): 799–814.

Oxford Dictionaries (2015) *Definition of discrimination*. [online] Available at: https://en.oxforddictionaries. com/definition/discrimination (accessed 23 June 2018).

Parris, M (2012) *An Introduction to Social Work Practice: A Practical Handbook*. Maidenhead: Open University Press/McGraw-Hill.

Pearson, G (1975) *Towards a New Social Work*. London: Routledge & Kegan Paul.

Rogers, C (1951) *Client-Centered Therapy: Its Current Practice, Implications and Theory*. London: Constable.

Ruch, G, Turney, D, Lymberry, M and Cooper, A (2010) *Relationship-Based Social Work: Getting to the Heart of Practice*. London: Jessica Kingsley.

Social Care Institute for Excellence (SCIE) (2010) *Personalisation: A Rough Guide*. [online] Available at: www. scie.org.uk/publications/guides/guide47 (accessed 23 June 2018).

Social Care Institute for Excellence (SCIE) (2015) *Co-Production in Social Care: What It Is and How To Do It*. [online] Available at: www.scie.org.uk/publications/guides/guide51 (accessed 23 June 2018).

Taylor, B and Devine, T (1993) *Assessing Needs and Planning Care in Social Work*. Aldershot: Ashgate/ Arena.

Taylor, C and White, S (2000) *Practicing Reflexivity in Health and Social Care: Making Knowledge*. Buckingham: Open University Press.

Tedam, P (2013) Developing Cultural Competence, in Bartoli, A (ed) *Anti-Racism in Social Work in Practice*. St Albans: Critical Publishing.

The College of Social Work (TCSW) (2012) *The Professional Capabilities Framework*. Now managed and delivered by BASW. [online] Available at: www.basw.co.uk/pcf (accessed 23 June 2018).

Thompson, N (2012) *Anti-Discriminatory Practice* (5th ed). Basingstoke: Palgrave: Macmillan.

Thompson, N (2015) *Understanding Social Work. Preparing for Practice* (4th ed). Basingstoke: Palgrave Macmillan.

Timms, N (1983) *Social Work Values: An Enquiry.* London: Routledge.

Tronto, J (1993) *Moral Boundaries: A Political Argument for an Ethic of Care* London: Routledge.

Whittington, C and Whittington, M (2015) Partnership Working, Ethics and Social Work Practice, in Bell, L and Hafford-Letchfield, T (eds) *Ethics, Values and Social Work Practice* (pp 76–89). Maidenhead: Open University Press.

Chapter 7 | Listening to Black students: A critical review of practice education

Su McCaughan, Gabrielle Hesk and Andrea Stanley

The authors would like to thank Suryia Nayak and Allison Coleman for their work in the development of the students' viewpoints

Introduction

Supporting Black students can be a challenging area of practice and, in presenting this chapter, we want to demonstrate that, despite having a cumulative 26 years between us as practice educators, we are still confronted by the unsettling realisation that we are not adequately supporting Black students in various practice settings. There is an inherent tension and fear of 'rocking the boat' when considering the competing pressures of retaining placements in a stretched social care arena and also being open to exploring the 'elephant in the room'. Our intention is to share our learning from our students' experiences and recognise the gaps we have found that are still present in practice education, both of which impact greatly on the experiences of Black students during their social work placement. Within the chapter we hope that you will be prepared to grapple with the 'thorny' issues that the case study explores, and engage fully with the reflective points that will help you to enhance your own practice, and draw you naturally into critical reflection.

Context

We are a Practice Learning Team based within a Social Work Directorate in a Higher Education Institute (HEI). As part of our role we prepare students across both undergraduate and postgraduate social work programmes for their assessed placement experience. The make-up of our student population is enriched by a diverse group of students from all over the world, the majority of whom are British citizens. In the academic year 2015/16 33 per cent of our social work students were from Black and Minority Ethnic (BAME) groups with that figure rising to 34 per cent in 2016/17.

Within this chapter we are questioning the endemic racism present within our society and its impact on the experience of Black students on social work programmes.

Although the majority of Black students on our social work programmes are British citizens there are wider considerations, as Hawkins (2017) states: *'Students from outside the European Union make up 60 per cent of entrants to postgraduate full-time taught master's degrees'*. International marketing strategies and partnerships encourage these numbers and attract students to join the UK HEI community and this in turn is reported to *'generate more than £25 billion for the economy'* (University UK, 2017). As we know, the kudos of an international link is held in high esteem and greatly considered within universities' strategic commitments, from international research to university world rankings. Within this chapter we begin to question the ethical and moral stance of universities working towards recruiting students from outside the European Union and their commitment to ensure that their experience of practice within the wider UK community is equal to that of the experience of white students. Research by Johnson (2016), *'addressing barriers to student success'*, names BAME students as one of the groups of students *'most affected by differential outcomes'*; this is heightened by factors such as poverty, disability and being older.

Miller and Donner (2000, p 34) state that it *'is imperative that when writing about issues of culture, race and/or ethnicity to first establish one's own cultural identity'*. As a staff team, we are a mix of ethnicities: one is Black British, three are white British, and one white Irish. We recognise that our own experiences of life and our identities, as well as gender, disability and sexuality, will shape how we respond to the students we support. Within this chapter we present a very personal and honest reflection of our learning and development as both individuals and as a team. We hope our sharing of this learning will assist other colleagues in practice education by offering a different lens with which to view this area of practice.

As part of the social work qualification students are assessed for 170 days in practice, divided across two placements. The student needs to successfully pass both placements to qualify and progress towards professional practice. Assessment requires a thoughtful and proactive approach from practice educators as passing or failing a student has a significant impact on all involved. Research into the impact on practice educators of failing a student is limited, but from our experience and ad hoc reporting, we have observed that the decision to fail a student has a long-term effect on many practice educators, at times affecting their decision whether or not to continue in this role as a practice educator. As with any assessment process, practice educators must be guided in their decision-making and should note possible bias within this process given the disproportionate representation of BAME students within the group of students who fail placement. Many students take the opportunity to repeat their placement at considerable personal and financial cost, the complexity of such situations being recognised and acknowledged. This is not a new issue and indeed has been the subject of discussion by others (Bartoli, 2013). However, listening to the students' voice ensures that, as a practice educator, we can tune in and respond to the challenge of supporting students more effectively alongside nurturing their professional development.

Case study

This case study explores the challenge of how the team responded to the reporting of racism by two Black African female students. The two students had been in a placement setting which had been quality assured by the university and had a tested history of student social work placements. Within our teaching we stress the importance of students listening to service users and carers to develop an understanding of their needs and to respect them as experts in their own lives. In the same way, we as educators must listen to students about their experiences on placement; but this time, listening was not enough – we needed to act and effect change.

We firmly believe that the experiences of students need to be heard and who better to seek this knowledge from but our students. The co-creation of the exploration and learning which took place between students and our team members has been an emotional, extremely important experience. We are keen to share this among the practice educating community with the aim of enhancing the placement experience for students. We confront the 'uncomfortableness' of racism, and power within the assessment process, using our combined knowledge and the shared experiences of our students.

The placement offered direct work with children and young people. Both students had been supported by an experienced off-site practice educator, and the on-site supervisor was an established team member within the agency. The agency had been quality assured as a first placement setting and increasingly students were able to engage in safeguarding work with vulnerable teenagers. Given that the placement engaged with our review process and made adjustments year on year, it was assessed as a quality practice learning experience.

On completion of the 70-day placement the students submitted an electronic evaluation of their experience. This tool aids in the evaluation of the student experience and includes: the allocation and induction process; support arrangements; accountability and role clarity; learning and assessment.

Feedback is quantitative with students being encouraged to include qualitative narrative accounts alongside this. Overall the two students rated their learning experience between good and excellent. However, their narratives provided a more detailed account of their experience; this included direct reports of racism. On being asked about the arrangement of having an off-site practice educator and an on-site supervisor, one student indicated '*I preferred speaking to an independent person*'. Both students highlighted features of racism – one described being excluded from professional forums including meetings and reviews regarding Looked After Children, '*due to discrimination*'. She noted that: '*This placement is actually a great learning tool overall in relation to building relationships and getting experience with children getting involved in child protection ... There also I feel is a culture within the placement to discriminate against people of colour and or different ethnicity as staff took a long time to acknowledge us or talk to us*'.

While it was evident that the non-Black students in the same setting reported difficulties with some elements of the placement, it was clear from analysing the responses that the Black students' race provided an additional layer of oppression.

This experience is linked to Crenshaw's (1989) theory of intersectionality. Carbado et al (2013, p 303) describe intersectionality as '*a method and a disposition, a heuristic and analytic tool*', which is '*rooted in Black feminism and Critical Race Theory*'. This perspective of intersectionality helps to explore the additional layers which can exist to further oppress people within our society, in this case the two Black female students. Crenshaw (1989) explores how the elements that we were aware of from the '*external representation*' based on their race, identity, skin colour, and gender worked against each other and against them, impacting on them receiving fair and equal supervision and support. Both students expressed concerns that the discrimination was on an organisational level, believing the staff team within the placement had developed a culture which was not welcoming to Black students.

Task 7.1

At this point it is worth pausing to think about how you currently/hope to address issues of intersectionality with your student. As a start consider when you have been treated as 'the outsider' (Smith, 1992). How did this feel and what did you do? You may have been in a gendered setting ... Then consider another moment of when you have considered someone else 'the outsider'? This may include, for example, making assumptions about someone based on age discrimination. Personal factors such as age, height, weight, cultural identity could be considered. Progress this further to think about your personal experiences with a student, acknowledging that each is unique but that the layering of each factor equates to intersectionality. Make a note of your thinking.

Drawing on the literature, Crenshaw (1989, p 140) challenges the notion that we can help forge change with our external voice on behalf of students, suggesting that utilising students' comments to raise our complaints and concerns is still not enough:

These problems of exclusion cannot be solved simply by including Black women within an already established analytical structure. Because the intersectional experience is greater than the sum of racism and sexism, any analysis that does not take intersectionality into account cannot sufficiently address the particular manner in which Black women are subordinated. Thus, for feminist theory and antiracist policy discourse to embrace the experiences and concerns of Black women, the entire framework that has been used as a basis for translating 'women's experience' or 'the Black experience' into concrete policy demands must be rethought and recast.

For the two Black students in this case study, neither student felt able to raise their concerns with either staff at the agency or with their tutor, practice educator or the academic lead within the placement team. This lack of reporting could be viewed negatively, as potentially being unable to challenge effectively, which could be linked to a student's ability to practice in the world of social work. If you are unable to raise concerns on your own behalf, how will you be able to safeguard others?! However, the students' experience highlights them being in a 'no win' situation. This is reinforced by Nayak (2017), who introduces the power of being silent or silenced in her work with women who have experienced sexual violence. Nayak suggests there is a recognisable thread which appears to be woven into the experience of racism, which our students have clearly experienced too:

Silence operates on an individual, family, community, societal and global level ... [it is a] clever tool for a number of reasons; Silence regulates and controls ... Silence shifts the shame and blame from the abuser to the abused ... Silence isolates.

(Nayak, 2017, p 10)

We are already aware from the research of Johnson (2016) that poverty and racism are often interlinked – translated this equates in practice – 'don't make a fuss or this will cost us'.

Task 7.2

Does this ring any uncomfortable bells? Have you any experience or observation of the dilemma that students may face? Should they raise an issue and suffer the consequences, for example, the worry of a placement ending or say nothing and to pass their assessment, but knowing the status quo will remain and nothing will change. Consider how easy it would be for students in your organisation to raise concerns? Make a list of the barriers that might prevent a student from voicing their concerns. Consider how you will take action and seek support for yourself.

Understanding that oppression can result in feeling silenced is hidden knowledge. Such knowledge derives from delving into the 'experience' of racism, facing the uncomfortableness and hearing the pain and observing the embarrassment. The activism of challenging of oppression by making 'political noise', such as attending protest rallies, can be more comfortable. However, as Nayak suggests the silencing is so powerful in the way it separates, divides and weakens people's experiences. It is no wonder that to conquer such silencing, individuals must become one, in order to be heard and make some noise. Although this is done with caution, and is a learned skill which is developed by one's lived experience of being Black, it can help to develop internal mechanisms, which dictate whether the risk of reporting racism is worth the potential consequences. All these elements, shifting and shaping, were experienced internally and negotiated daily by these two students, alongside their learning, their ability to grasp and understand the concepts of the social work framework for assessment (Professional Capabilities Framework), to learn ways of working with service users and to link theory to practice. This seems an additional challenge alongside navigating their experiences of racism and discrimination.

Task 7.3

Now can you begin to comprehend the additional layers? Intersectionality shows us how the weight and experience of these additional layers has an impact on BAME students. As a practice educator you could well have been involved in political action but now we ask you to consider the more personal zone. How would you respond or support a student who is experiencing being treated as outsider?

Responding to concerns – reports of discrimination

The students' experiences concur with those reported by Thomas et al (2011, p 37), who evaluated a pilot study of a mentoring scheme to support BAME students on placement. They found that research indicated *'that progression and retention rates for students from marginalised groups is lower than the sector averages and that specific support systems can improve the likelihood of course completion, as well as increasing student confidence.'*

In their analysis, Thomas et al (2011) draw on Rowe (1990, p 160), who likens the impact of being made to feel an outsider in joining a new group as *'a dripping tap'* effect *'whereby students are subjected to different treatment, for example, irritation in the tone of voice being used, being ignored within the team, or not greeted as other members of staff are'*.

The feedback from the two Black students affected the Practice Learning Team in different ways and created different responses. We have since reflected on this as a team, acknowledging our own differences and how it impacted on each of us. On reviewing the feedback from the students there were emotions from the team of feeling shock and dismay. The academic who arranged the placement felt personally responsible for the students' experience, given their responsibility for the development of the setting over several years. There was an immediate acknowledgement that this was racism and needed to be addressed rather than buried. Other members of the team felt too close in terms of their lived experience, and were not shocked. The danger in this was acknowledged, ie the silencing of Black students could also be experienced by their Black educators, and hence a resistance to face the situation head on or feel unable to effect change based on past experiences. This led to reflections as a team on our differences and perspectives on the situation; some felt keen to respond immediately, others sat back and reflected and others began to support colleagues by offering to assist in looking at ways to understand this. The strength of the team and their ability to grapple with the issues honestly resulted in a full team approach to ensure that we were proactive and not silent.

The two female students were invited to meet with a member of the team, to explore their comments and both welcomed the opportunity to talk about the issues they had raised. Both were certain that they had made the right decision to complete the placement rather than flag up the concern, based on their judgement that it was likely their placement would have been terminated early. Bartoli et al (2008) highlight the increasing number of Black African students who fail the practice component of their qualification, which is mirrored in the experience of students at our HEI. The two students highlighted issues of power imbalance in the assessment process, to the extent they felt unable to raise the issues with their practice educator or any university staff. They supported each other throughout their placement, acknowledging that this helped, but seeing another student being ostracised due to their race and skin colour only added to the harrowing experience.

Echoing Rowe's (1990) research, one student stated:

I felt oppressed in my placement as even before I came it was not fully explained what to do if you are discriminated against due to race or bullied. I have also watched another student be discriminated against.

Both students considered they had little choice but to continue with the placement and achieve the end goal of completing 70 days of practice without drawing attention to themselves. They considered it inappropriate to challenge the agency staff or to raise the issues with the practice educator or academic staff. Again, this concurs with Bartoli et al's (2008, p 84) findings of the *'perceived deference Black African students believe they should demonstrate to those in authority, (including academic tutors and team managers) which is further compounded by the traditional deference expected from women steeped in patriarchal ideology and dominance'.*

Task 7.4

The Mandela Model is a tool that has been created specifically for use in the supervisory relationship between student and practice educator (Tedam, 2011). This is an excellent tool to explore the specificity of identity and cultural difference within the practice learning supervisory role. Consider the supervisory relationship with your student and use the Mandela Model to guide you. Note any action points including arranging to talk to other practice educators about their experiences.

The 'elephant in the room': Reflecting on the impact of race in education and practice

As practice educators we are always encouraged to consider the core values of our professions whether it be social work, nursing, or any other allied health and social care profession. The expectation of valuing the students we educate must be high on our agenda throughout the placement period. The inclusion of race, culture and identity is crucial to the relationship between the practice educator and the student. Acknowledging this at the beginning of the relationship in your supervisory agreement is necessary as it enables you to return to identified issues and explore any uncertainties which emerge along the placement journey. The power imbalance must be understood in all contexts and shared honestly with the student. Thus, the ownership of the introduction to this exploration must lie with the practice educator, however uncomfortable it may be.

Task 7.5

How do you explore power relations with your student? When is the right time? Is this aspect of your relationship discussed with the student at the beginning of the placement? Is it included in your supervision agreement? Do you make reference to codes of conduct within these discussions? Do you return to this agreement throughout the placement to review whether it is working for you both? The discussions around power and oppression should become deeper and more meaningful as your relationship with your student develops.

Using your professional code of conduct not only helps us to remind students what they will be expected to adhere to when they enter the profession, but it also allows you and students to use these as points of reference in their reflection and academic work.

Based on our combined experiences of practice, as students, as practice educators and as academics and through listening to the lived experiences of our students, we embrace how difficult it may be to introduce discussions on these topics. Acknowledgement of power in relation to race, gender or class is hard to broach, especially when working in such a diverse field as health and social care. This may be particularly pertinent if the practice educator has little experience or indeed when the student and the practice educator do not share the same identities. We know that it can be a complex topic to understand and to know how to open conversations and that sometimes this can lead to complacency or even ignoring areas which need clarity such as race, culture, identity, disability, sexuality.

However, we also acknowledge that supporting individual students will be different each time and we cannot be complacent, expecting that treating everyone in the same way is sufficient or fair. When it comes to issues such as race and identity we must adapt, revisit and refresh our thinking regularly. There are intricate elements within a person's culture and identity that need to be explored and cannot be duplicated and applied in the same way with each student. As mentioned earlier, their personal experience, based on features including skin colour, skin tone, ethnicity, accent, facial features, hair type, cultural linguistics, will all affect the way in which people are treated within society, and within practice, and ultimately if they are to be accepted. However, if we are to better understand the nuances of racism and offer students appropriate support these elements need unpicking.

Task 7.6

Think of the practice placement as a microcosm of society in general. Revisit your social work practice in terms of ethics and values. Consider principles of respect and the impact of small acts of kindness on each other. Develop and note some actions points for your next student supervision session.

We know that discrimination and racism can be present within all our lives, cultures and upbringing, without us even knowing it. Social work education is well known for considering these elements, helping students to self-identify where the subtlety of racism can spill over into our everyday lives, and can be easily considered as 'the norm' of one's cultural ideology. These ideologies which are created and shaped by these elements in our lives can tend to creep back in through the cracks of complacency or when we feel threatened. The danger is that this complacency can become the 'norm' again, as we revert back to the safety of what we grew up with or how we were taught. The 'norm' is what we as practice educators must understand and be clear about within our roles as educators as it is this honesty which helps us to formulate our own ways of working.

The following quote from Lorde resonates with us and reiterates the need for us to grapple and stay with this self-reflection:

I urge each one of us here to reach down into that deep place of knowledge inside herself and touch that terror and loathing of any difference that lives there. See whose face it wears. Then the personal as the political can begin to illuminate all our choices.

(Lorde, 1979, p 101)

Task 7.7

Considering Lorde's quote above, think back to your own education, that moment when you question yourself, or someone close to you, based on what you have read, heard, learned, or listened to in a lecture or book. Recall the 'uncomfortableness' and the realisation, that what you have learned, done, been taught as a child, may have been wrong, may have been offensive, may be inflicting pain on an emotional level, to someone else. Dig deep! Sharing this honestly with your student may be one way of encouraging them to open up and discuss difference. The Johari window (Luft and Ingham, 1961) would be a useful tool to open up a reflective discussion.

We need to ensure that practice educators who are training work hard to uncover and discuss any of these differences in working with students. It can be a challenge to make time for this, especially if you are a practice educator immersed in practice yourself or an off-site practice educator with many students to support. Another difficulty to consider is noted by Rooks (2014), who states:

Far too many of us consider the act of discussing structural racism to be racist in and of itself. It's a problem in society and it's a problem in the academy, [HEI's] too.

Therefore, we need to ensure that we create an environment from the outset, which ensures BAME students are able to feel at ease to share their 'lived' experience and feel able to express these without fear of retribution, which could impact on the assessment of practice. This environment needs to acknowledge the element of power which is present and can often become a barrier to open discussion in the student/ practice educator relationship.

Hill Collins (2000, p vii) reminds us of the need to consider:

... the complexity of ideas that exist in both scholarly and everyday life and present[ing] those ideas in a way that made them not less powerful or rigorous but accessible. Approaching theory in this way challenges both the ideas of educated elites and the role of theory sustaining hierarchies of privilege.

The blind spot – cultural assumptions and how to create change

In Bellack's (2015, p 63) paper she refers to Banaji and Greenwald's (2013) perception of the blind spot, in relation to our 'unconscious bias'. This involves discussing the areas of ourselves that we are not yet aware of, that *'operate as hidden blind spots, ones that are difficult to see and which we are unaware yet influence our beliefs about and behaviour towards others'*.

Task 7.7

This leads us beautifully into our suggestion that you read Peggy McIntosh's (1989) 'White Privilege: Unpacking the Invisible Knapsack' and consider using this as a reflective tool which could be used on a one-to-one basis with your student or with your colleagues as an exercise aimed at developing together their understanding of oppression. It will hopefully encourage discussion and expression, and demonstrate that you as a practice educator are open to learning that there are differences between each one of us.

Within our own case study our immediate response was to talk with the students and then approach and challenge the practice setting; however, our overwhelming concern was whether this was a hidden issue and that as an HEI we had been culturally blind to the 'lived' experiences of BAME students.

Zevallos (2011) draws on Essed's (1991) research into everyday racism experienced by Black women to argue that *'the power of othering includes opting out of "seeing" or responding to racism'* (Zevallos, 2011). This was our fear and we were concerned that we had not addressed the issue of race and 'otherness' directly with other placement settings and felt we too had been part of the institutional racism inherent in our society. The two students could have approached the Practice Learning Team, removed from the direct assessment triangle, and able to be utilised for guidance and external support. Their reluctance to do so concurs with Maundeni (1999) and the characterisation of the African female university student's reluctance to ask for support to increase their understanding of the curriculum.

This knowledge sat uncomfortably with our growing evidence that a number of Black students were failing the practice module and, in particular, how a number of agencies opted to withdraw their support for the student on placement rather than working towards a clearly evidenced fail or offering a robust opportunity to be tested in practice with a positive outcome. This links to the 'hidden processes' which Bernard et al (2011, p 7) refer to in their research exploring the particular circumstances of Black and ethnic minority and disabled students to identify the specific factors that contribute to their experiences while on social work programmes. The cumulative effect of intersecting disadvantage, for example, students who have dyslexia, Black and ethnic minority students with financial as well as caring responsibilities, meant certain students were particularly vulnerable to the fear of delayed progression.

As part of our response to the issue of racism we sought guidance from our student network with the aim of listening more closely and learning from their experiences on placement. We collaborated with the student network to develop an equality and diversity survey which asked specific questions of students on their experiences on placements, for example:

» How would you describe the atmosphere towards you personally while on placement?

» Do you feel that you were treated unequally while on placement?

» Do you feel there were any factors about you personally which contributed to it?

These factors included gender, ethnicity, class, disability, personal appearance, age, accent, the way I speak, and caring responsibilities. We also asked for qualitative comments regarding any unequal treatment experienced while on placement. Of the 39 responses, seven responses were attributed to race, five to age, five to accent, three to disability, three to personal appearance and five were other comments which included the experience of feeling excluded from learning opportunities, not receiving information about cases or personal development, being ignored in training spaces, public criticism, difference in tone of voice used when being addressed. The majority of all respondents reported talking about difficulties to friends, family, practice educators and tutors; however, six students stated they did not report issues due to not wanting to disrupt or endanger the placement. Just over half (55 per cent) of all respondents reported a lack of discussion about equality issues within the placement environment. These results suggest that there is a lack of awareness of inherent racism on the part of those working in practice.

Surprisingly, the findings from the student survey were not as strongly indicative of what we anticipated. This may link with what Bernard et al (2011) refer to as students will only consider sharing their critical analysis of experiences of race if they feel represented, listened to and taken seriously, resulting in changes in practice.

As a team we felt that the process had been cathartic for the students involved and, based on their feedback, that they and we as lecturers had also learned an immense amount from listening to students. The ability of the students to be able to speak out about their experiences was crucial and the fact that we as educators encouraged them to share and flip the roles by the students becoming the educators was important to them and empowered them to speak.

> ## Reflective point:
>
> *Think about the principle of learning from each other. How do you actively engage in collaboration and partnership with your student? Think about how to begin an open conversation about equality and how the student will raise issues within the placement and what they may hide, for fear of 'rocking the boat'.*
>
> *Draw up a section to address this within your induction phase. Building on your understanding of 'white privilege', Bartoli et al (2015, p 246) ask us to consider this from other angles within academia, such as counselling and psychotherapy programmes.*
>
> ... white privilege is often designed to address the needs of minority populations, and it rarely places Whiteness in the spotlight. Its structure, in fact, risks mirroring the very dynamics embedded in white privilege ... which has a profound impact on the quality of communication and interaction within and across racial groups ...

Sharing messages – challenge and change

In responding to the concerns of our two Black female students, and in asking further questions of our student group, we had started to hear some important messages. The messages impacted on us all in different ways but, for all of us, they began to promote deeper reflections and a recognition that we need to create and encourage opportunities for open and honest dialogue between practice educators and Black students. We were conscious of the fact that, as a team of academics who are all engaged in practice learning, we have opportunities to involve ourselves in dialogue and peer reflection, but that these opportunities are not so regularly available for practice educators in other settings. We therefore wanted to share the powerful messages from our students in a forum that would provide an opportunity for other practice educators to hear the voice of Black students.

We invited a small group of Black students to work in collaboration with us to present their narratives in a workshop at a specialist conference for the training and development of practice educators called the National Organisation for Practice Teachers England (NOPT). While facilitated by members of the Practice Learning Team, the workshop was developed and led by the students themselves. The overarching aim was not only to promote the experiences of Black students but to improve the confidence of practice educators in listening to and working with Black students.

Bartoli et al (2008) found that while practice teachers were experienced in supervising staff and students, they were relatively inexperienced in supervising Black students. Students in Bartoli et al's (2008, p 85) study reported *'being covertly discriminated against and "oppressed", being monitored more closely than other white students, to the extent that their progress was hindered'*. We therefore considered that influencing practice educators through the workshop might lead, indirectly, to a positive change within practice settings, promoting change, as well as addressing issues directly concerning placement settings. We were mindful that participating in such a conference was likely to attract a certain type of practitioner, ie a reflective practice educator, as the workshop attendance was self-selecting, attracting those who have a more positive attitude to anti-oppressive practice and development. However, we were motivated to start somewhere; even starting small would help us to engage more fully with the emerging challenge.

In preparing for the workshop, we asked the small group of students to identify issues that they believed had significantly impacted on their experiences on placement. One of these areas was communication, and the students' response to this is presented as an example of how accepting the invitation to see things through their 'lens' can be a powerful tool for change (Hesk, 2017, p 198). A regularly reported aspect of communication on placement was the lack of understanding that some individual students experienced due to their accent or use of articulation. A number of Black students had been told that their accent was not understood and they needed to learn to speak more clearly. However, in our discussions with them they told us that they, too, often struggled to understand their white colleagues' accents. A number of students raised the issue of English not being their first language and at times they were marginalised by the fast pace of 'office chatter'. Differences in regional dialogue were also confusing. However, white colleagues were never told that they should try to speak more clearly! Although the students in our group came from a diverse range of backgrounds, they all agreed that if they struggled to understand a white colleague's voice they were unlikely to have the confidence to say this and so may misinterpret what was being said or miss key bits of information. This resonates with the findings of the study undertaken by Fairtlough et al (2013), where some students reported that negative assumptions were made about their African accents. To highlight this within the workshop, practice educators were asked to repeat a phrase and this was passed around the room. The accents were varied and included a range of regional English accents, Scottish, Irish and African voices. The message was simple: *'it's not just us that's different: we're all different!'* The impact of this exercise was evident and the two students leading the discussion were able to identify that struggling to understand and be understood is a barrier to effective and open communication, particularly at the beginning of placement. However, the key message here is that communication is a two-way process and may require change from both parties.

> ### Reflective point:
>
> *Think about the make-up of your team. What regional accents or dialects are reflected among team members? What phrases or accents might confuse a student whose first language is not English?*

We were keen to provide practical insights into placement issues, so the workshop participants were asked to think of one thing that they would like to ask the students and to consider questions that may well be 'the elephant in the room'. Students had also identified key areas that they wanted to raise with the group, with themes including the ability for practice educators to give constructive criticism and provide good use of supervision including meaningful and clear discussion about feelings. Messages from this discussion included the need for open and honest dialogue which was built on a foundation of mutual trust and respect. While this is true of any practice educator/student relationship, the students' testimonies illustrate the need for a reciprocal relationship which the practice educator listens to and acknowledges the world the student inhabits. This is particularly important when providing feedback to the student or identifying areas for improvement.

During placement, several of the students had been labelled as 'struggling' and as having 'poor communication skills'. To see them in the workshop expressing themselves clearly, assertively and with confidence was a powerful experience for all and highlighted the racist ideologies which shaped and formed such negative labels. Valuing them as 'experts by experience' gave us a further perspective on the challenges they faced.

The emotional impact of listening to this group of students was immense for all participants present, and feedback from seasoned practice educators was that they valued the opportunity to honestly explore the 'elephant in the room' and not to be fearful of this. This was surely a transformative experience for all involved. Knott and Scragg (2013, p 43) state that *'there is increasing recognition of the role of emotion in critical thinking and deep learning'.* Engaging with the concept of emotion let us consider reflection in our own practice as well as our students.

Reflective point:

Can you think of anything that you would change with regard to communication with your student? Maybe you could review how well things are working with your student during the lifetime of the placement, rather than at the end. Be open to any critical learning from this and try not to fear change, as change and adaptation is good practice.

Our aim for the workshop was to facilitate an open and frank exchange and that by listening to the students' voice practice educators would positively modify their practice and so enhance the experience for future students. The session concluded by asking participants to identify areas for change within their practice and feedback from this exercise reinforced our belief that listening to the narratives of Black students was a powerful catalyst for change.

Our team want to ensure that the impact of the experience of listening to Black students results in action that is embedded in our teaching and learning activities. Subsequently, we have purposefully taken what we have learned from the Black student voices into the education and training of future practice educators, within continuing professional development (CPD) workshops and mentoring support, with the aim of creating spaces for dialogue. Our direction has provided more depth and focus and brought equality and diversity into a more open and honest domain. Feedback indicates that this has led to a wider understanding of the need for openness around cultural issues.

We have also linked our classroom teaching, focusing on preparation for placement to include direct discussion on inequality and its possible impact on students. By raising awareness of introducing these issues and procedures to follow it up, it is hoped that students will be more open in reporting back to the Practice Learning Team any need for support. Our aim is to encourage and empower students to speak out at the earliest opportunity, to highlight and resolve issues of inequality and oppression. Feeling better prepared by opening up the conversation hopefully equates to a more positive student experience. The next step for us is to reach a wider audience by developing what we have learned. We intend to create a video which allows Black students to teach students and professionals about their personal experiences. This could be used as a tool to open up dialogue in the placement setting.

Creating forward change

In conclusion, there is an overarching need for practice education to consider the student experience and long-term consequences of the impact of racism or any other form of discrimination. If we fail to do this we are in danger of creating a workforce of social workers who never gain the opportunity to deal with the complexity of feelings which are required when understanding the use of self in contemporary practice. As social workers we need to be able to understand our own needs and rights and be able to articulate them. If we are not supported to develop these skills as part of our journey of lifelong learning, we are unlikely to transfer these skills to our work with service users.

Our experience has confirmed to us that part of the practice educator's role is to support students to voice their concerns and anxieties around placement issues. Building on this, the practice educator needs to value the dialogue which comes from these discussions and enable a two-way learning process whereby the practice educator's understanding of race is enhanced. In essence, this would be similar to any other link to the Professional Capabilities Framework (PCF) domains. In the light of this the task of confronting racism would be located within the supervisory relationship, rather than being the responsibility of the student.

It is not possible to allocate practice educators with students from similar cultures, nor do the students we collaborated with consider this is the best way to encourage change. Practice educators can develop openness to discuss an array of challenging issues including race and discrimination and encourage openness from the student learner. By drawing out the student's skills, strengths and previous experience the practice educator can learn from the student and ensure they feel supported to be honest about their placement experience. The most powerful tool that the practice educator can use to support a student is to listen to what is being said, clarify what is being said and then take action.

As a group of practice educators, we recognise that the majority of our learning in this area comes from the students we work with, and thus they need to be valued as a 'live' resource, while encouraging us to be open to shared learning.

As a team this has led to a process of transformative learning and encourages us to be open to collaborative working. It has begun to shape our practice and we hope it will have a positive impact on the student experience.

References

Banaji, M R and Greenwald, A G (2013) *Blindspot: Hidden Biases of Good People*. New York: Delacorte Press.

Bartoli, A, Kennedy, S and Tedam, P (2008) Practice Learning: Who Is Failing to Adjust? Black African Student Experience of Practice Learning in a Social Work Setting. *Journal of Practice Teaching*, 8(2): 75–90. Doi:10.1921/81134

Bartoli, A (ed) (2013) *Anti-Racism in Social Work Practice*. London: Critical Publishing Ltd.

Bartoli, E, Bentley-Edwards, K L, García, A M, Michael, A and Ervin, A (2015) What Do White Counsellors and Psychotherapists Need to Know About Race? White Racial Socialization in Counselling and Psychotherapy Training Programs. *Women and Therapy*, 38(3–4): 246–62.

Bellack, J (2015) Unconscious Bias: An Obstacle to Cultural Competence. *The Journal of Nursing Education*, 54(9): S63–4. doi:10.3928/01484834-20150814-1

Bernard, C, Fairclough, A, Fletcher, J and Ahmet, A (2011) *Diversity and Progression among Social Work Students in England*. London: Goldsmiths, University of London.

Carbado, D, Crenshaw, K, Mays, V and Tomlinson, B (2013) INTERSECTIONALITY: Mapping the Movements of a Theory. *Du Bois Review: Social Science Research on Race*, 10(2): 303–12.

Crenshaw, K (1989) Demarginalizing the Intersection of Race and Sex: A Black Feminist Critique of Antidiscrimination Doctrine, Feminist Theory and Antiracist Politics. *University of Chicago Legal Forum*, 1989(1): Article 8. [online] Available at: http://chicagounbound.uchicago.edu/uclf/vol1989/iss1/8 (accessed 23 June 2018).

Essed, P (1991) *Understanding Everyday Racism: An Interdisciplinary Theory*. Sage Series on Race and Ethnic Relations (vol 2). Newbury Park, CA: Sage.

Fairtlough, A, Bernard, C and Ahmet, A (2014) Black Social Work Students' Experiences of Practice Learning: Understanding Differential Progression Rates. *Journal of Social Work*, 14(6): 605–24.

Hawkins, R (2017) *The Changing Face of International Student Recruitment*. 14 March. [online] Available at: http://blog.hefce.ac.uk/2017/03/14/the-changing-face-of-international-student-recruitment (accessed 23 June 2018).

Hesk, G (2017) Gather in My Name, My Skin, My Everything... (Gather in My Name: Maya Angelou). Special edition: Bordering, Exclusions and Necropolitics. *Qualitative Research Journal*, 17(3): 142–54. https://doi.org/10.1108/QRJ-08-2017-089

Hill Collins, P (2000) *Black Feminist Thought: Knowledge, Consciousness and the Politics of Empowerment*. London and New York: Routledge.

Johnson, K, (2016) *A Waste of Talent and Potential*, 26 August. HEFCE. [online] Available at: http://blog.hefce.ac.uk/2016/08/26/a-waste-of-talent-and-potential (accessed 23 June 2018).

Knott, C and Scragg, T (2013) *Reflective Practice in Social Work*. London: Sage.

Lorde, A (1979) The Master's Tools Will Never Dismantle the Master's House. Comments from the Personal and the Political Panel (second *Sex Conference*, October 29 1979).

Luft, J and Ingham, H (1961) The Model: The Johari Window Model. *Human Relations Training News*. [online] Available at: https://c.ymcdn.com/sites/fridayfellowship.site-ym.com/resource/collection/D1FD72B3-693E-4EE5-AB18-B1233BBE9C51/JohariWindow_JLuft.pdf (accessed 23 June 2018).

Maundeni, T (1999) African Females and Adjustment to Studying Abroad. *Gender & Education*, 11(1): 27–42.

McIntosh, P (1989) White Privilege: Unpacking the Invisible Knapsack. *Peace and Freedom Magazine*, July/August: 10–12. [online] Available at: www.ywca.org/atf/cf/%7B6EDE3711-6615-4DDD-B12A-F9E0A781AE81%7D/White%20Privilege%20Unpacking%20the%20Invisible%20Knapsack.pdf (accessed 23 June 2018).

Miller, J and Donner, S (2000) More Than Just Talk: The Use of Racial Dialogues to Combat Racism. *Social Work with Groups*, 23(1): 31–53.

National Organisation of Practice Teachers England (NOPT). [online] Available at: www.nopt.org (accessed 23 June 2018).

Nayak, S (2017) Declaring the Activism of Black Feminist Theory. *Annual Review of Critical Psychology*, 13: 1–12. [online] Available at: http://usir.salford.ac.uk/43761 (accessed 23 June 2018).

Rooks, N (2014) *Why Can't We Talk About Race?* 4 March. [online] Available at: https://chroniclevitae.com/news/367-why-can-t-we-talk-about-race (accessed 23 June 2018).

Rowe, M (1990) Barriers to Equality: The Power of Subtle Discrimination to Maintain Unequal Opportunity. *Employers Responsibilities and Rights Journal*, 3(2): 153–63.

Smith, D (1992) Sociology from Women's Experience: A Reaffirmation. *Sociological Theory*, 10(1): 88–98.

Tedam, P (2011) The MANDELA Model of Practice Learning: An Old Present in New Wrapping? *Journal of Practice Teaching & Learning*, 11(2): 60–76. doi:10.1921/ 175951511X661219

Thomas, G, Howe, K and Keen, S (2011) Supporting Black and Minority Ethnic Students in Practice Learning. *Journal of Practice Teaching and Learning*, 10(3): 37–54.

University UK (2017) *International Students Now Worth £25 Billion to UK Economy – New Research*. 6 March. [online] Available at: www.universitiesuk.ac.uk/news/Pages/International-students-now-worth-25-billion-to-UK-economy---new-research.aspx (accessed 23 June 2018).

Zevallos, Z (2011) *What is Otherness?* [online] Available at: https://othersociologist.com/otherness-resources (accessed 23 June 2018).

| # Supporting students with dyslexia on placement: Theory into practice

Rachael Hunt and Ian Mathews

There are potentially many issues concerning the health and well-being of students that may come to the attention of practice educators either before or during the placement period. Placements are often the first time that many students, some of whom are young and with limited life experience, have engaged with the complexity of other people's lives and the demands of professional practice. Consequently, it is not unusual for the demands of being on placement, and the pressures that experience generates, to exacerbate or even create issues which need to be sensitively addressed by both practice educators and universities.

Universities differ in their approach to disclosing pre-existing health, learning or well-being issues to placement providers, and often feel constrained by legislation and internal policies which may limit the information they feel able to share with external parties. In turn, some students are reluctant to disclose health, well-being or learning issues to their university as they feel that this will have adverse consequences for them; specifically that it will jeopardise their chances of getting a placement (McPheat, 2014). Students are not legally obliged to disclose that they have any issues, and HCPC guidance simply states that students may 'consider' telling their education provider about any additional needs they may have (HCPC, 2015). On occasions this can lead to real difficulty as practice educators find themselves without any opportunity to prepare either themselves or the placement that they are working with students with complex needs. Sometimes 'reasonable adjustments' under the Equality Act 2010 may be required, flexibilities introduced, and the placement reconfigured in order to meet the needs of students. While this scenario is rare, it can create real difficulties for placement providers and adversely affect relationships between universities and providers.

Task 8.1

Often students feel overawed coming on placement and can be cautious about disclosing that they may need additional support. How would you approach such a student? Importantly, how would your team and your line manager respond?

Sometimes team culture is extremely supportive and accepting of 'new learners' but other teams can, at least at first, be unenthusiastic.

This chapter focuses on supporting students with dyslexia and describes how one university has assisted practice educators to work with dyslexic students. We are anxious not to catastrophise this condition and want to state at the outset that dyslexia should not be an insuperable barrier to the profession and that many people with dyslexia make excellent students and practitioners. It does, however, need to be recognised and understood as it may create difficulties to learning on placement.

Dyslexia

Dyslexia is a complex, and contested term and it is outside the scope of this chapter to offer an analysis of the evolving construction of this term. For the purposes of this chapter we adopt the following definition from the British Dyslexia Association (2007):

Dyslexia is a specific learning difficulty that mainly affects the development of literacy and language related skills. It is likely to be present at birth and to be life-long in its effects. It is characterised by difficulties with phonological processing, rapid naming, working memory, processing speed, and the automatic development of skills that may not match up to an individual's other cognitive abilities.

Interestingly, there has been very little research into the impact of dyslexia on the social work profession, and the literature relating to any of the caring professions is limited. This is surprising as anecdotally there is a suggestion that people with dyslexia are over-represented in the care sector as other professions and areas of work are denied them and that the personalised nature of care plays to their many strengths. Equally, given the requirements of the profession that social workers record, present and analyse significant amounts of complex information, often under pressure and against demanding timescales, it is perhaps unexpected that the issues associated with dyslexia have not received greater prominence.

The British Dyslexia Association suggest that 10 per cent of the population are dyslexic, although this figure is open to challenge as dyslexia is often a hidden undiagnosed condition. For example, universities are often surprised at the number of students who have successfully passed through their school years and entered higher education only to discover during the course of their studies that they have dyslexia. There are, of course, good reasons why some students may wish to hide their difficulties and many of them are adept at creating coping strategies which mask the extent of their difficulties.

Recent studies of student nurses have suggested that 12 per cent of undergraduate nursing students have dyslexia (Wray et al, 2011; Evans, 2015) and that this figure is rising (Evans, 2014a). Less recent research indicates a figure of 5 per cent, although this discrepancy may be due to a greater contemporary awareness and an emphasis on widening participation among further education institutions (Wright, 2000; Illingworth, 2005). Typically, these studies identify potential difficulties regarding the safe administration of medication (White, 2007), the completion of patients' records, remembering verbal instructions, accurately completing reports and remembering names (Illingworth, 2005). While these professional concerns should not be underestimated, it is also important to recognise that many nurses with dyslexia bring strengths with them to the workplace, not least excellent personal skills, creativity, and an empathic understanding of the needs of patients. Goldberg et al (2003) identified a range of attributes common to adults with dyslexia which assist them to lead a successful life. These include self-awareness, perseverance, flexibility and the effective use of coping strategies.

Task 8.2

Like many areas of difference or disability, dyslexia is often portrayed as being a problem both to the individual sufferer and to any potential employer. Thinking about the breadth of social work and social care practice, and the wide range of skills and insights required to be an effective practitioner, can you identify any aspects of practice where the attributes identified by Goldberg et al (2003) would be an asset?

Given the paucity of research into social work and dyslexia, it is difficult to make comparisons with nursing or to offer an analysis of the impact of dyslexia. What we do know is that social work students with a 'self-declared disability' are more likely to fail to complete their studies, or to be delayed, than students without a learning issue (Moriarty et al, 2009; Evans, 2014b). Similarly, social work students with dyslexia are less likely to obtain a good degree compared with those with no declared learning issue (Hussein et al, 2008). Anecdotally, it is also suggested that a disproportionate number of students with a diagnosis of dyslexia enter the concerns process during their placements.

Given these areas of concern, and a consistent message from placement providers that they wanted more support in assisting students with dyslexia, the University of Lincoln practice team decided to investigate the number of students who had a diagnosis of dyslexia and how they and their practice educators might be better supported while on placement. In the academic year 2016/17 across the undergraduate and Masters in Social Work programmes, 30 students out of a total of 171 had a diagnosis of dyslexia. This equates to approximately 18 per cent of the overall cohort. Similarly, between the academic years 2014/15 and 2016/17 the number of students across the School of Health and Social Care (which delivers degrees in nursing, social work, and health and social care) with a Learning Support Plan for dyslexia had nearly doubled. While it is difficult to extrapolate with any degree of certainty using these figures, it does demonstrate that a significant number of students on the social work degree programmes, and other allied programmes, have dyslexia.

Task 8.3

Do these figures surprise or even shock you? Why do you think that the number has doubled in recent years? The answer to these questions is probably quite complex, but may be indicative of greater awareness and better methods of diagnosis.

Supporting students with dyslexia on placements:

In partnership with the university well-being centre, students and practice educators, the practice team developed and introduced two guides aimed at assisting both students and practice educators to recognise and work effectively and successfully with the strengths and limitations inherent within dyslexia. In order to help us to discuss our work with practice educators, significant sections of the guide for placement staff can be found below. As can be seen, the guide offers a brief overview of dyslexia and details what support can be provided by the university to students. It then alludes to reasonable adjustments before discussing the following aspects of dyslexia:

- » Memory and processing
- » Motor skills and co-ordination
- » Communication
- » Reading
- » Literacy

Each of these potential characteristics are discussed, with particular reference to issues which might arise on placements, and strategies which might help or be discussed are suggested. Please read the guide and gain an understanding of how it could be used in your work as a practice educator or placement provider. We will then conclude our chapter by making some observations about the use of the guide by practice educators.

THE DYSLEXIA GUIDE FOR PLACEMENT STAFF

WHAT IS DYSLEXIA?

The British Dyslexia Association defines dyslexia as:

... a specific learning difficulty that mainly affects the development of literacy and language related skills. It is likely to be present at birth and to be life-long in its effects. It is characterised by difficulties with phonological processing, rapid naming, working memory, processing speed, and the automatic development of skills that may not match up to an individual's other cognitive abilities.

It can affect an individual's:

> » reading, spelling and writing;
> » numeracy skills, such as making calculations, mental arithmetic, and times-tables;
> » getting organised, meeting deadlines and personal organisation;
> » memory;
> » sequencing, such as getting dates and numbers in the right order;
> » concentration.

It is considered a general term for disorders that involve difficulty in learning to read or interpret words, letters and other symbols, but do not affect general intelligence.

It is worth noting that there is not just one definition for dyslexia. Dyslexia affects around one in ten of us, and often presents itself in various different ways. Every person with dyslexia is unique; however they may share similar characteristics, and may experience issues with:

> » their *'short-term memory (or working memory), which may not be as efficient as that of individuals without dyslexia;*
> » *their speed of processing information may be slower than for those without dyslexia'* (Godwin, 2012)

The British Dyslexia Association website holds a lot of information about dyslexia and offers advice on various aspects for students and assessors: www.bdaDyslexia.org.uk/

Many students will be aware that they have dyslexia prior to enrolling at university; however, some may find that the support services available at the university help to identify issues that they have been struggling with. The university has a successful support system in place, which is very accessible. Please see page 4 for further information on these services.

A main component of a student's degree within the School of Health and Social Care will involve an assessment of competencies on placement. Students may find that their dyslexia presents in a different way when it comes to placement; it is therefore encouraged that students share any difficulties with the placement team and the staff supporting them on placement. Sharing this information offers the placement and the staff supporting students an opportunity to discuss the support that can be offered, along with what support the student requires. It is essential that the student and the placement are aware of the expectations of one another to allow for a supportive environment which will offer the individual the best learning opportunity.

This guide has been put together to explain the support on offer through the university to students with dyslexia. It also includes strategies which students and placement staff have used in the past to ensure that a placement learning opportunity has been successful with the right level of support on offer for the student.

SUPPORT TO STUDENTS WITH DYSLEXIA

The university has a Student Wellbeing Centre which has a dedicated team who are able to support students with their learning needs. The Wellbeing Centre discuss student specific needs in relation to academic support as well as placement-specific support. The team will develop a Learning Support Plan with the student. This plan, with the student's permission, can be shared with the placement itself.

During the students' placement application process, students are asked if they have a Learning Support Plan and to detail any strategies that they have in place which will help them to manage their specific learning needs throughout the placement. There is an area for students to indicate whether there are additional measures which they think will help to support them during their placement period. Students choose whether or not they wish to share this information with the Student Wellbeing Centre, their placement support team at the university and their placements; students are strongly encouraged to share these details, as this allows for reasonable adjustments to be made within the placement, should it be required.

Placements have a responsibility to provide opportunities for all students, regardless of gender, age, ethnicity, or disability. It is illegal for placements to discriminate against a student with a disability. It is expected that placements will make reasonable adjustments (defined on page 6) to allow for students to be placed and to access successful learning opportunities.

It is also expected that students take responsibility for their own learning and where possible discuss their specific learning needs at their pre-placement meeting or where possible to allow the placement to support the student.

There are a number of ways in which a student declares their learning needs, including:

- » during a university open day – face to face;
- » during the application process;
- » drop-in sessions with the Student Wellbeing Centre on a one-to-one basis;
- » disclosure (self-assessment) forms.

There are a number of support systems in place for use during placement; these are identified on a Learning Support Plan:

- » Where possible, a student can be provided with a USB version of TextHelp Read and Write to assist them with reading and understanding information while on placement.
- » Where confidentiality allows, a student can take their digital recorder into placement.
- » Additional time and assistance (if required) with reading essential placement-based information.
- » It is recommended that you have any written documentation proofread; please approach your placement assessor or personal tutor for advice and support.

If issues arise within the placement environment which relate to a student's dyslexia then a concerns process can be initiated. If a meeting is held to discuss these concerns and it is felt appropriate, then a representative from the Wellbeing Centre can be invited to advise and offer recommendations.

The Student Wellbeing Centre also offer telephone support to students if they are on placement. Contact details are included at the end of this guide.

Some placements themselves may have a dyslexia policy; it would be useful to look through this at the earliest possibility.

The Student Wellbeing Centre holds drop-in services:

Monday–Friday 12–2pm and on Thursday an additional drop-in session is held from 5pm. Times may vary outside of term time; these times are announced on the service's Facebook and Twitter pages:

www.facebook.com/uniofLincolnSWC
www.twitter.com/UniofLincolnSWC

and are also circulated via student email.

It is essential that placement staff are able to assess all students at the same level, with the support, strategies and reasonable adjustments in place.

REASONABLE ADJUSTMENTS

Reasonable adjustments are a key part of the Equality Act 2010, and are defined within Chapter 2, section 20 of the Act, which can be found here. It is expected that any placement supporting a student, who has declared that they have a disability, makes reasonable adjustments. These reasonable adjustments will support the student with their learning and development and will allow for practice assessors to assess the student's competencies in a supportive environment.

There are opportunities for students throughout their placement processes to declare their disability and to discuss strategies and progress. The university encourages students to share their needs with the university, the Student Wellbeing Centre and their placement as soon as possible. We also recommend that any student-specific needs are discussed at interviews or pre-placement meetings with their placement assessors; this gives an opportunity for students and placements to plan for the placement period as well as offering an opportunity for the placement assessors to provide any useful reading in advance, which will give the student time to process any crucial information.

Dyslexia can present itself in a number of ways; it is worth noting that adjustments which have been made for one student may not work as well for other students. These differing aspects of dyslexia may include difficulty with:

> » Memory and processing
> » Motor skills and co-ordination
> » Communication
> » Reading
> » Literacy

In addition, students may be impacted emotionally by their dyslexia, and may struggle with self-confidence. This can affect their performance within the placement environment; this highlights the importance of providing an environment that supports and develops the student to the best of their ability. Providing such an environment will assist with the student's confidence and will also offer practice assessors an appropriate, learning opportunity, in which a student can be assessed.

It is unusual that students with dyslexia will have difficulties in all of these areas; however within this guide we have addressed each area individually and suggested strategies which can be used in some instances. As stated above each student with dyslexia is unique, and therefore some strategies may be successful with one student, but not with another.

MEMORY AND PROCESSING

Students with dyslexia may experience difficulties linked to memory and processing, these include:

- » short attention span and distractibility;
- » ordering their ideas;
- » remembering names, job roles, contact details, telephone messages and placement-specific terminology;
- » retaining information – including instruction and observations taken;
- » organisational difficulties which may affect searching for information alphabetically, organising workload and commitments and multitasking;
- » processing written information, including dates, times, appointments, and contact numbers;
- » communicating accurate messages verbally with colleagues;
- » following set tasks in the correct sequence, which might affect their ability to learn routines and interventions quickly;
- » ability to manage the balance between Academic and Practice elements of the course;
- » time allocation for specific tasks and being able to complete them within expected timeframes;
- » responding appropriately and within a timely manner where the demands of placement are more urgent;
- » having a clear idea of their responsibilities and expectations.

Strategies for practice assessors:

» Develop a plan for the placement period at the beginning in collaboration with the student, to include vital information such as:

Important meeting dates, measurable learning outcomes against competencies required, expectations of the student and the placement, information regarding the building and environment (including maps where necessary), placement/induction packs.

» Provide additional time to discuss routines and administrative procedures.

» Explain tasks more than once, in a clear way, with both written and verbal instruction where possible.

» Provide numerous opportunities for students to observe yourself and other practitioners during contact with service users; encourage the student to discuss and reflect on what they might do.

MOTOR SKILLS AND CO-ORDINATION

Students with dyslexia may experience difficulties linked to motor skills and co-ordination, which include:

» learning how to undertake specific sequences or interventions, due to processing and retaining information;

» motor skill co-ordination difficulties related to the right and left-hand side of the body;

» handwriting documents in a clear and orderly manner.

Strategies for practice assessors:

» Repeat demonstration of skills on more than one occasion to embed learning.

» Where suitable allow student opportunities to practise skills.

» Closely supervise practice until the student is confident.

» Tools or aids – such as diagrams or flow charts.

» Allow students extra time when writing up documentation.

COMMUNICATION

Students with dyslexia may experience difficulties linked to communication, which include:

» expressing ideas clearly;

» learning and remembering practice-based language and terminology;

» understanding long complex instructions;

» staying focused when giving clear instructions;

» finding the correct words to use;

» understanding the meaning of words which have more than one meaning.

Strategies for practice assessors:

» Use aids or tools which can support with terminology; where appropriate allow students to record specific language and terminology on paper or using a dictaphone.

» Provide written information which details any abbreviations or terminology that may be used within the placement period.

» Ensure instructions are given clearly.

» Provide feedback in a direct manner, using clear statements.

» Repeat instructions given and welcome any questions.

» Ask student to repeat terminology and/or instructions to embed learning.

READING

Students with dyslexia may experience difficulties linked to reading, which include:

» skimming or scanning text;

» reading out loud;

» pronouncing terminology, placement language or unfamiliar words;

» reading text on white backgrounds, for instance on white boards, computer screens or in documents;

- » understanding charts/tables which include information presented both vertically and horizontally;
- » reading accurately when coming to words they are unsure of;
- » recognising, mispronunciation, and misinterpretation of information;
- » reading in loud busy environments with distractions;
- » distinguishing between two words which look familiar.

Strategies for practice assessors:

- » Offer students a quiet area for them to process the information they are required to read.
- » Offer lots of opportunities to discuss and reflect on information the student has read.
- » Give the student extra time to read, if required.
- » If there is a lot of background reading or recommended reading to complete, provide the student with a lot of notice.
- » Inform the student of main areas of text that might be useful.
- » If using whiteboards, use colour to highlight areas and to reduce confusion.
- » If writing documents for students, ensure that information is presented in clear structured sentences; for main areas of interest use bullet points, or highlight information; and try not to use abbreviations or placement-specific language

LITERACY

Students with dyslexia may experience difficulties linked to writing and spelling, which include:

- » the spelling of placement-specific language and terminology;
- » scanning or skimming documentation;
- » summarising information;
- » writing and spelling correctly when under time constraints;
- » presenting documents in an orderly way with clear handwriting;

» completing placement-specific forms accurately;

» remembering sequences and ordering them correctly, for example phone numbers or abbreviations;

» distinguishing between two words which sound the same;

» using the correct language and terms;

» transferring their thoughts onto paper accurately;

» writing in a clear and concise manner.

Strategies for practice assessors:

» Give students extra time to write up placement documents, for example forms, reports and case studies.

» Allow students to take notes, where appropriate, and write them up neatly later.

» Proofreading the students' placement work.

» Provide examples of reports and other placement documents, to give the student an idea of format and language that should be included.

» Point out main areas that students should focus on when writing up documents.

» Allow students to record data in flow charts or tables.

» If appropriate, allow students to type on coloured backgrounds with fonts that are clear and simple.

FEEDBACK FROM STUDENTS AND PRACTICE ASSESSORS

During the process of putting this guide together, the practice placement team have liaised with students and staff involved within placements. Many of them suggested similar strategies to those listed above which they found useful during placement. However, some suggested specific techniques that they found extremely helpful; these included:

» allowing extra time when writing reports/case notes;

» arranging proofreading of documentation with placement support staff;

- » creating a calendar with important dates highlighted – such as submission dates, reflective journal review dates, learning agreement and midpoint review dates, and supervision dates;

- » creating an A–Z book which holds key terminology, user names and reminders;

- » requesting a quiet space to carry out complex phone calls, writing up case notes/reports;

- » writing down key words from assessment criteria to assist with understanding, creating visual aids with key words;

- » using different colour paper and overlays;

- » ensuring that they write clear notes from supervision sessions, which have clear headings and action points;

- » creating a diary, which is updated with supervision dates, deadlines and goals;

- » discussing support needs from the pre-placement meeting and throughout the placement to ensure that all staff are aware of what is needed and can make reasonable adjustments;

- » making supervision sessions practical;

- » repeating information within supervision and ensuring that things are covered thoroughly;

- » using a dictaphone where appropriate (consider confidentiality throughout placement if this is to be used);

- » develop a routine within the placement, allowing flexibility;

- » discuss early on their preferred working methods with placement staff and university support.

If you are able to discuss these ideas with your student, they may be able to develop their own list of helpful techniques which will make the most of their practice learning opportunity.

The placement team welcome your advice and would appreciate any further techniques which you have found useful when supporting students. You may wish to include some further advice in this guide to support other students and placement assessors. If you do think of a strategy that you use successfully during placement which has not been covered – please get in touch.

Conclusion

As can be seen, this is a practical document which offers straightforward advice and guidance across a range of issues pertinent to practice educators supporting students with dyslexia. The final section detailing feedback from students and practice educators is particularly valuable as it provides an insight into practical considerations adopted by placements.

Consistent feedback from practice educators has confirmed that they have found the guide to be useful and that it has encouraged them to adapt aspects of their practice.

The guide has also been used as a tool to openly discuss dyslexia and the support needs of students. As we know, sometimes talking about disabilities, particularly those which are hidden, can be problematical and having the guide as a starting point has been useful. Interestingly, a number of practice educators also have a diagnosis of dyslexia and the guide has served to stimulate reflection on their experiences of undertaking the social work degree, sometimes with little support, and the issues they have encountered as practitioners.

Placements additionally reported that they felt more comfortable about referring students back to the university for support and guidance because the guide provides information on what support services may be available. This has been helpful as sometimes there is a disconnect between placements and universities with busy practice educators being unclear what, if anything, universities can offer to students.

While it would be unwise to overstate the significance of this guide, placements do value clear communication with universities regarding their work with students, especially those who may be seen to be different. It would also be unfair to stigmatise students with dyslexia as the overwhelming majority make excellent practitioners and enhance the profession.

We hope that this guide goes some way to enable students to fulfil their undoubted potential and assures agencies that they can offer outstanding placement opportunities to students with dyslexia.

References

British Dyslexia Association (2007) [online] Available at: www.bdadyslexia.org.uk (accessed 23 June 2018).

Evans, W (2014a) If They Can't Tell the Difference Between Duphalac and Digoxin You've Got Patient Safety Issues. Nurse Lecturers' Constructions of Students' Dyslexic Identities in Nurse Education. *Nurse Education Today*, 34(6): 41–46.

Evans, W (2014b) 'I Am Not a Dyslexic Person I'm a Person with Dyslexia': Identity Constructions of Dyslexia Among Students in Nurse Education. *Journal of Advanced Nursing*, 70(2): 360–72.

Evans, W (2015) Disclosing a Dyslexic Identity. *British Journal of Nursing*, 24(7): 383–85.

Goldberg, R, Higgins, E, Raskind, M and Herman, K (2003) Predictors of Success in Individuals with Learning Disabilities: A Qualitative Analysis of a 20-Year Longitudinal Study. *Learning Disabilities Research and Practice*, 18: 222–36.

Health and Care Professions Council (HCPC) (2015) *Health, Disability and Becoming a Health and Care Professional*. London: HCPC.

Hussein, S, Moriarty, J, Manthorpe, J and Huxley, P (2008) Diversity and Progression among Students Starting Social Work Qualifying Programmes in England between 1995 and 1998: A Quantitative Study. *British Journal of Social Work*, 38: 1588–1609.

Illingworth, K (2005) The Effects of Dyslexia on the Work of Nurses and Healthcare Assistants. *Nursing Standard*, 19(38): 41–48.

McPheat, C (2014) Experience of Nursing Students with Dyslexia on Clinical Placement. *Nursing Standard*, 28(41): 44–49.

Moriarty, J, Manthorpe, J, Chauhan, B, Jones, G, Wenman, H and Hussein, S (2009) 'Hanging on a Little Thin Line': Barriers to Progression and Retention in Social Work Education. *Social Work Education*, 28(4): 363–79.

White, J (2007) Supporting Nursing Students with Dyslexia in Clinical Practice. *Nursing Standard*, 21(19): 35–42.

Wray, J, Aspland, J, Taghzouit, J, Pace, K and Harrison, P (2011) Screening for Specific Learning Difficulties: The Impact Upon the Progression of Pre-Registration Nursing Students. *Nurse Education Today*, 32(1): 96–100.

Wright, D (2000) Educational Support for Nursing and Midwifery Students with Dyslexia. *Nursing Standard*, 14(41): 35–41.

Index